DRIVEN

JAMES MARTIN

Driven

COOKING IN THE FAST LANE – MY STORY

Collins

James Martin asserts his moral right to be identified as the author of this work.

A catalogue record for this book is available from the British Library.

ISBN-13: 978-0-00-729467-1

Set by Rowland Phototypesetting Ltd, Bury St Edmunds, Suffolk
Printed and bound in Great Britain by Clays Ltd, St Ives plc.

Picture acknowledgements: **p1** (top left) Susan Martin;
(top right) Peter Smith Photography; (bottom right) Peter
Smith Photography; **p2** (left) UKTV; **p3** (bottom) Chris
Capstick/BBC; **p4** (top) BBC; **p5** Sally Kettle; **p6** (left)
Greg King/BBC; (right) Sally Kettle; **p7** Sally Kettle;
p8 Telegraph Media; **p9-16** Sally Kettle.

While every effort has been made to trace the owners of
copyright material reproduced herein, the publishers would
like to apologise for any omissions and will be pleased
to incorporate missing acknowledgments in
any future correspondence.

Mixed Sources
Product group from well-managed
forests and other controlled sources
www.fsc.org Cert no. SW-COC-1806
© 1996 Forest Stewardship Council

FSC is a non-profit international organisation established to promote the
responsible management of the world's forests. Products carrying the FSC
label are independently certified to assure consumers that they come
from forests that are managed to meet the social, economic and
ecological needs of present and future generations.

Find out more about HarperCollins and the environment at
www.harpercollins.co.uk/green

This book is dedicated to all the people
I've met, **loved**, lost, *punched*, argued with,
KICKED, sworn at, bought from, sold to, *hired*,
sacked, **spoken about**, WRITTEN ABOUT,
fallen out with, hated, worked with
and ***had a drink with***. You have
shaped my life and this book.

CONTENTS

INTRODUCTION

Most people probably don't know about my car obsession, but it's quite serious, and I've had it a long time. From my earliest memory, my life has been dedicated to the pursuit of two passions – cooking and motors. To be honest, I can't remember which came first; the two have always gone hand in hand. As a kid, I was either helping out in the kitchens of Castle Howard, where my father was catering manager, or driving a tractor around the fields of our farm. If I wasn't flambéing chicken livers at catering college, I was circling Golf GTis in *AutoTrader* and dreaming of Ferraris. And if I wasn't working 18-hour shifts in some of the most punishing kitchens in London, I was spending what little I'd earned on some ridiculous kit car with no roof and big shiny exhaust pipes. Every job I've ever had has been to finance wheels of some description. I know that most people associate me with cooking, but for people who really know me, cars are probably the first thing that spring to mind. Put it this way: I've got a beautiful big kitchen at home, but my garages, all three of them, are more impressive. My whole life has been wrapped up with cars in some way. Knowing that, it's easier to understand why this has been one of the most monumental years of my life. This year has seen the realisation of one of my dreams. This year I took part in the world's ultimate road race.

I was just 22 when I first heard of the Mille Miglia road race, a 1,000 mile rally through the medieval streets and squares of Italy, from Brescia to Rome and back again. At the time, I was head chef at the Hotel Du Vin in Winchester and was constantly surrounded by mega-rich people with mega-money cars. I'd just acquired a fantastic little two-seater kit car of my own, so when I overheard talk about a world-famous classic car race, my ears pricked up. Not long after, I came across an article about it and from there I was hooked.

Enzo Ferrari called it 'the world's greatest road race'. Only in Italy would they allow three hundred vintage sports cars to drive at breakneck speeds on public roads, competing against one another and against the clock, cheered on by women, children, young men, old men, local mayors and the police. It's fast, loud and dangerous, and utterly intoxicating. I read about the Mille Miglia's glory days when Juan Manuel Fangio and Stirling Moss battled it out, Moss ultimately claiming triumph in 1955 in his legendary Mercedes-Benz 300SLR, completing the race in a staggering 10 hours 7 minutes and 48 seconds. I read about the horrific accidents, including the one that killed twelve spectators in 1957 and led to the annual event being scrapped on grounds of safety. Then I read about the race's 1982 revival as an historic rally for vintage cars, a time trial rather than an out-and-out race. I wanted to go and see all the incredible machines, to hear the noise and feel the excitement. Right then and there I promised myself that one day, if it was the last thing I did, I would go and watch the Mille Miglia.

I never in my wildest dreams thought I'd actually get to drive in the thing. That seemed such an impossibility that it wasn't even an ambition. Back in its heyday, if you were able to get hold of a car and some petrol, you could be out there going wheel to wheel with Moss and Fangio. Technically, it's still open to anyone. Every year roughly two thousand people apply to take part in the race. Only around 350 are chosen, and it's all based on the eligibility of the car. You can't buy or muscle your way into the Mille Miglia, you have to be invited once you've applied. On the upside, that means it's not full of rich brats and yuppies with too much money and no idea of style and sophistication. On the downside you need bags of money, because eligible cars don't come cheap, and neither does getting them to the start ramp.

Fast-forward to 2005 and I was at the BBC to talk about a new cooking series. We were trying to brainstorm ideas but not coming up with anything. As an aside I mentioned the forthcoming Mille Miglia and how I would love to go to watch it because I was nuts about cars. Suddenly everyone in the room perked up and wanted to know more about the race and my car collection. They asked me to write a proposal for a programme based around my actually doing the race.

I had no idea what the proposal should look like, so I got in touch with a producer I knew. He said that the best thing to do wasn't to try to put the race on paper, but to put it on film, to make a mini pilot so the BBC could get a feel for the cars, the places, the event. So two weeks later, there I was, standing next to the start ramp in Brescia, a camera in my face, shouting above the roar of an Alfa Romeo revving up behind me, 'Forget Monaco, forget Formula One, this is the most amazing race in the world, the Mille Miglia, and next year I'm going to do it.'

A week after they got the pilot, the BBC came back with a yes. And that was it. I was doing the Mille Miglia. Not that any of us – me, the production company, the BBC – had even the first clue how to go about it. Production hired someone to sort out the logistics of the race, the application process, and everything related to the organisation of the race itself. The BBC set a budget but it was barely enough to cover the camera crew and the editing, so the car and a co-driver were most definitely going to have to come out of my own pocket. In fact, money got so tight so quickly that when it became clear I was going to have to hire support mechanics too and pay for their transport, food and accommodation I struck a deal with the producer. I said, 'I'll waive my fee if you pay for the support team.' He agreed, no doubt thinking he was getting the better deal, but for once being paid nothing really did make sound financial sense. Not that earning nothing and borrowing vast sums of money to pay for cars I really can't afford was anything new to me. Throughout my life I've seemed to make a habit of it, though I've never once had any regrets.

There were moments when I wasn't convinced I was ever going to make it to the start line. At one point my car, a bright red 1948 Maserati A6GCS, one of only three made that year by the legendary Italian car manufacturer, looked worryingly like a two-year-old's Lego set, i.e. in pieces, and lots of them. The bills for repair were adding up and the loan I took out in the first place to cover buying the car and getting it into the race was already bigger than the mortgage on my house. At one point the loan repayments alone were more than I used to earn in a year at Hotel Du Vin, when I first read about the race. But if it's your dream, you've got to do it, right? For once, I actually agree with my dad, who always used to say that anything in life is possible, it just depends whether you're prepared to work hard enough for it. And I'd worked hard for this. I'd spent my whole life working towards this point, absorbing everything there was to know about cars, hurtling through my life on four wheels and using all my hard-earned cash to fuel my passion. And now I can truly say that nothing comes close to the noise of thousands of over-excited Italians screaming and cheering as the cars throttle down the famous start ramp and charge off into the night, down the narrowest of cobbled streets, made narrower by the devoted crowds that line the way from start to finish – and this being Italy, there are no barriers separating cars and spectators; they don't even close the roads for it. It's the biggest collection of classic cars you'll ever see, not sitting in a museum gathering dust but out on the road doing what they were built for. This three-day test of skill, stamina and decades-old metalwork is the ultimate adventure for any car fanatic. And I'm utterly proud that I've been a part of it.

Cars and food might not be an obvious combination to most people, but to me it all makes perfect sense. One just always seems to lead to the other and, as you'll see, I've gone to ridiculous lengths for both. So while it may come as a surprise to hear me raving on about vintage cars and Italian rallies, rather than celeriac mash and spun sugar, you should know that every memory of every job, pay packet, place and person I can think of comes with a make and model number attached. Looking back, it's easy to see how everything I've ever done has been leading me un-swervingly to the start line of the world's most famous road race. I hope the stories that follow will show you why entering the Mille Miglia has meant so much to me, and that you'll enjoy reading about some of the best moments of my life.

1 SKATEBOARDING AROUND THE KITCHEN TABLE

It all started when I was seven years old. I was skateboarding around the kitchen table. I remember going round and round. I couldn't get enough of the speed, the challenge, the skill, the going round and round.

We lived in an old farmhouse with a big kitchen which was always at the centre of everything. The kitchen was the hub of the family as well as the house. It was all pine inside, with a huge dresser, a big old butler's sink and a big round pine table with pine chairs. The table sat ten and was always busy. People didn't knock on the door of our house, they just walked straight into the kitchen and made themselves at home. It was a lovely place to be. That's where my love of food started. If my mum wasn't cooking, my dad was. Mealtimes were a big deal in our house, and Sunday lunch was the most important. The table would be packed for it. My grandparents would be there, my mum, my dad, my sister, my aunty, and me, on my skateboard.

As well as the big pine table, the other important feature

of the kitchen was a big old Aga with a metal towel rail on the front of it. If you pulled on the towel rail quickly enough while stood on a skateboard, you could launch yourself with enough force to ride almost all the way round the kitchen table. What made the kitchen particularly suitable for skateboarding, though, was the floor. It had these cork tiles which with hindsight were horrible but at the time were perfect for skateboarding on. Ceramic tiles or lino would have been lethal: one pull on the Aga towel rail and you'd have been off with a broken neck. But the cork tiles, designed to stop nasty slips while holding a boiling pan, gave all the grip you needed for a successful run around the kitchen table.

Skateboarding was the 'in' thing at the time. Me and my mates were all into it, but me being me I couldn't just have a normal skateboard. Firstly, I was very particular about which one I had. If I asked for a skateboard for Christmas I was very specific. Normal kids would write in their letter, 'Dear Santa, please bring me a skateboard'; I would write, 'Dear Santa, please bring me a skateboard, model XT47, blue, available from Halfords, priced £14.99.' That way I'd be sure I was getting the right one. And it had to be the right one. I didn't want a red one or a black one or a yellow one, I wanted a blue one. I didn't want an XT20 or an XT40, it had to be the XT47. And if my granny asked my mum what I wanted, there was always the outfit to go with it. I had the full gear – the knee pads, the arm pads, the helmet.

Our little farming village had never seen anything like it. I looked a right pillock going down the road, slowly, on my skateboard dressed head to toe in all the get-up. I don't think any of the other kids in the village had seen anything like it either. Me and my best mate David Coates used to skateboard together, but his wasn't as good as mine because he would just write 'skateboard' on his list for Santa. David used to be way better than me at almost everything we did, but he never quite had the right gear. He may have been better at sport than me, but he never looked quite as good doing it. Yes, there was intense competition to have the best skateboard, the coolest BMX. It was like real life Top Trumps back then. It still is now, only with Ferraris.

Getting the right board and outfit was only the start of it though. I could never leave it as the standard board everyone else had, I had to 'trick' mine. It's always been the way, no matter what I've owned: I've got to modify it, make it better. So every penny of the pocket money I used to earn mowing the lawns, doing a bit of gardening or helping out on the farm mucking out the pigs went on 'improvements'.

We weren't proper farmers, of course. With my dad's catering manager post at Castle Howard came a house and some land which was pretty much useless for anything other than farming, so at various times we had pigs, cattle and chickens which me and my sister Charlotte, who's a year younger than me, used to help out with. It wasn't highly paid work – we were only seven and six – so when you spent you had to spend wisely. At the corner shop my 50p pay would buy me a Coke and a Mars bar (twice) and a handful of Floral gums. I hated Floral gums. They were, and still are, disgusting. They tasted like soap, but they were the only sweets my sister didn't like, which made them good value. She'd have all the good sweets, which I'd nick off her; I'd have all the crap ones, which she wouldn't come near. They might not have been pleasant, but they made the most of the money.

With only limited funds and a standard skateboard in need of 'improvement', some particularly creative thinking was required. I could work all year and I still wouldn't be able to afford the proper (and eye-wateringly expensive) foot grips they sold in Halfords, so I cut two feet-shaped pieces out of some sandpaper in my dad's shed and glued them to the top of my board with UHU. Careful saving of my hard-earned fifties meant I could just about afford the four new wheels I wanted – one red, two white, one blue – and, most important of all, the special tricked-out ball bearings required to do all the proper stunts. The only problem was, I couldn't ride the bloody thing. I could barely stand up on it, never mind do stunts. I used to have to sit on it on my bum to go down hills. Which is why I did most of my skateboarding in the kitchen.

So there I was in the kitchen, in all the gear – knee pads, arm pads, helmet – looking like a pillock, holding on to the towel rail of the Aga. It was a Sunday lunchtime and everyone was in the kitchen, sitting round the table, which I was launching myself around again and again, making everyone dizzy and increasingly irritated. My grandfather was getting particularly annoyed as I tried, and more often than not failed, to circle the ten seated obstacles.

Of everyone around that table, my grandfather, my

mum's dad, was the least likely to put up with such antics. A former cricketer, a fast bowler, he used to play for Yorkshire with Freddie Trueman, he worked as a ticket man on the railway and was a proper no-nonsense Yorkshireman who didn't really make allowances. He used to say things like 'Get a proper job, play cricket.' When we used to 'play' in his back garden, which always featured an absolutely perfect cricket pitch lawn, stripes and all, he'd bowl cricket balls at me at 150 miles an hour, overarm, like he was warming up against Botham in the nets. You learned quickly to give the ball a good hit to show you were trying, but not too hard because you knew that if you really whacked it and it went over the hedge the next ball would be coming straight at your head. Needless to say, I hate cricket.

So, everyone was chatting away, trying to ignore me but getting more and more annoyed as I went round and round, almost but not quite making it all the way round the table because, maybe, someone had pushed their chair out and I've crashed into it. On my fourth or fifth attempt, my grandfather had finally had enough.

'So, son,' he said with a force that put me off what could have been my first full flying lap of the day, 'what do you want to do when you get older?'

I stopped my skateboard right next to him and without even thinking about it I replied that I wanted to be a chef.

My dad, being a catering manager, knew a thing or two about chefs and he was nodding and saying, 'That's all right that. Good career. Hard work, but a good career.' Granddad wasn't looking quite so impressed, but spurred on by my dad's approval I added, 'I want to be a head chef at 30, have my own restaurant at 35 and have a Ferrari when I'm 40.'

My granddad turned to me, a look of disgust on his face, and in his firm Yorkshire accent he said, 'You want to get a bloody proper job, play cricket. You'll never get all that, not being a chef.'

Now, anyone who knows me will tell you that I'm not one to shy away from a challenge. They'll also tell you that I'm the hardest-working person they know. All my friends will say that I put in more hours, more effort and more passion than anyone else they've ever met and that if I say I'm going to do something, I usually do it. Even so, through all the years of working 18-hour days, living on the bread-line, begging, borrowing and stealing (literally) to survive, standing up to jumped-up little French chefs, being battered and abused in restaurant kitchens over the years, being ripped off in business and being mistaken for a fool more than once, I would never in my wildest dreams have imagined the truth: that I'd achieve all the boastful ambitions I voiced as a seven-year-old on a skateboard by the time I was 24.

2 ARCADE GAMES AND ASTON MARTINS: THE V8 VANTAGE

Scarborough, 1979. I'm in a 'Kiss Me Quick' cowboy hat, eating pink candyfloss, walking along the seafront with my mum, my dad and my sister, and I'm having a lovely time. It's grey and windy and the only thing moving on the beach is the rubbish and the poor old 10p-a-ride donkeys, but it doesn't matter.

We went to Scarborough a lot when I was a kid, at week-ends and during school holidays, so much so it's a wonder that eating all those whelks and pickled herrings and pots of winkles in vinegar – the ones you ate with a plastic fork – and the tons of sticky rock (which for some reason wasn't the traditional pink stick kind but made up to look like a plate of sausage, bacon and eggs) didn't leave me scarred for life. Thankfully I only have happy memories of our trips to the seaside, not least because it was on that grey and windswept east coast seafront that I discovered two of the greatest passions of my life.

At the time, I thought Scarborough was one of the best

places on the planet. I know now that although it can be fun, it can also be one of the most boring places. I mean, the Labour Party hold their conference there. I just remember it being bloody cold and grim at times, with one solitary speedboat that went up and down and a funfair that hardly ever used to be open because it was either too windy or pissing down with rain. And it hasn't changed to this day: it's still your typical sleepy seaside town full of old dears and the faint smell of wee and Dettol. But back then, to a young lad with a pocket full of hard-earned and carefully saved 50ps, it was magic, full of excitement. Typically, my sister used to blow all of her money in the pound shop as soon as we got there; she'd come out with rolls of clingfilm and 15 teddy bears, thinking she'd got a bargain. Me, I headed straight for the bright lights and endless pleasures of Scarborough's only real saving grace, the amusement arcades.

Then as now, Scarborough's seafront was crammed with huge arcade houses, and I used to spend hour after hour in them. That's where I started my lifelong obsession with those fairground grabbing games, the ones where you have to pick up the cuddly toy or some other bit of tat with a pincer on a hoist. Whenever I see one I have to have a go on it, and once I've started there's no getting me off. I've been known to put £65 in one of those things at a time and walk away with nothing but a smile to show for it. Then again I don't smoke and I don't drink – well, not much – so I figure I'll play on the grabby games if I want to.

Of all Scarborough's arcades, there was one in particular

that was always guaranteed to excite a young man looking to put his hand-eye coordination to the test. The biggest, most glitzy arcade on the front (well, it looked glitzy to me at the time) had this huge sign of red mirrored discs which used to glitter in the wind with the words 'Henry Marshall' in massive gold letters that lit up at night. It was a Mecca for excitable small boys like me with change in their pockets, and it was outside there one day when I was off to try my hand at grabbing something cheap and tacky that I discovered the other great obsession of my life.

There, right outside Henry Marshall's amusement arcade, on a double yellow line, was a brand-new, shiny, British racing green Aston Martin V8 Vantage.

Now, I'd spent enough time in the back of my dad's less than sporty MkI Escort playing 'Spot the Car' with my sister – 'that's my car, that's your car, that's my car ...' – to know a good car when I saw one, and I knew this was something else. It wasn't just a brand-new Aston Martin, it was the Prince of Wales edition, with the V8 engine. Even then I could spot the V8 because it had different wheels and wider wheel arches than the standard one. To buy that car today would be expensive, £200,000 at least; back then it would have been astronomical. We're talking a lottery money motor. Pure hand-built luxury. British racing green, chrome everywhere, soft top, cream leather interior with green piping, a private number plate – it looked the business. Absolutely amazing. And there was something about the fact that it was parked on the double yellow that made it even better. What did the owner care about parking tickets?

He had an Aston Martin V8 Vantage Prince of Wales edition. He could afford to pay the fines.

I stood there gazing at it in awe, my 99 Flake dripping down my fingers. I was standing on tiptoes trying to get a proper look inside while my dad tried to drag me away, terrified that I was going to get Mr Whippy all over the paintwork. Like all the other dads of all the other kids who had suddenly surrounded it and were clawing for a better look and getting fingerprints and candyfloss all over it, my dad was desperate to prise me away from the window before the owner came back. There were kids everywhere shouting, 'Dad, Dad, have you seen this?' 'Dad, Dad, what is it?' 'Dad, Dad, how much is it?' 'Dad, Dad, can we get one?' while their embarrassed fathers tried to distract them and get them as far away from the vehicle as possible ... until, that is, the owner's 20-something girlfriend with never-ending legs and the shortest miniskirt you've ever seen came tottering along on her high heels and climbed into the passenger's seat. Suddenly the dads weren't in such a hurry to leave and it was the mothers who were insisting it was time to go.

Next thing, the car's owner – and putting two and two together this must have been Henry Marshall himself because there couldn't have been too many other people around those parts who could afford a car as spectacular as that – came out, made his way through the crowd, got in, fired it up – oh, the amazing roar of the V8! – then without so much as a wheelspin gracefully took off down the road.

I'd never seen anything like it. It was magic. I had been

brought up with tractors and farm animals; you just didn't see a thing like this every day. It was a defining moment. The one that makes you choose either women or cars (although it also made me realise that if I could afford a car like that, I could afford a girl like Henry Marshall's to go with it). So I chose cars.

3 BOYS' TOYS

Flying isn't really my thing. I'm not a big fan. I see it just as a necessity, as a way to get from A to Z without trekking all the way round the rest of the alphabet. Sometimes, flying is essential, but don't ask me to like it. I'd rather drive. Now there's a surprise.

I'm sure many factors have influenced my dislike (or should I say mistrust) of aviation, but the one that springs immediately to mind is my very first flight. It was not a pleasant experience. To be honest, it was heartbreaking and more than a little embarrassing.

The whole family had come to watch. It was a pretty big occasion on account of the fact that I'd made quite a big deal of it, told everyone they had to be there to witness the event. So there they all were, the entire family, gathered round to show their support and see a very young me take to the skies on his maiden voyage. Instead they got to witness the horror of my plane dropping from the sky like a stone just seconds after take-off, hurtling towards the ground, and crashing into a million little pieces – well, two big ones.

I'd spent about two months and all my pocket money building that bloody thing. It was a big two-channel remote control glider, the kind you launched with a piece of elastic on a hook. The idea was that you attached the little hook underneath to the piece of elastic which you'd wind up and then release, launching the glider into the air. You'd then fly it around working the rudder and ailerons with the remote control. At least that was the idea. Didn't really work out that way on my first flight.

The family were assembled in the farmyard round the back of our house to see the big launch. My dad was winding the elastic and I was on the controller ready to steer it around the skies of North Yorkshire as soon as it was airborne. My dad was winding like a madman, checking with me all the time.

'Ready? Ready?' He wound some more. 'Ready?'

'Yep, ready!'

And with that it was off. My mum was squealing, 'He's built it, it's flying, look everyone, it's flying!' like it was the Wright Brothers' first flight or something, my dad was fit to collapse after all the winding, I was on the controller and, BANG!, it was on the ground in two very broken pieces. The bloody elastic hadn't detached, so the plane went straight up and straight back down again. All those months of gluing together those bits of wood and stretching that plastic skin over the wings and shrinking it on with a hair dryer, all that for nothing. There in front of an audience of my nearest and dearest I had to go and pick it up and carry it back to the shed.

The humiliation.

However, never let it be said that I'm not determined. Not to be defeated, I went straight out and bought a bigger, better one, white with an engine included this time. Exactly the same thing happened. I spent months and months and all my pocket money on building the thing, took it out back to the hard standing we had where we used to put all the lorries and tractors, started it up, and it took off and just nose-dived straight back down again. After that it was years before I mustered up the courage or enthusiasm to have another go. To be honest, it's only now that I'm just about starting to get the hang of it. I try because I hate giving up, but deep down I know flying really isn't my thing.

Remote control cars, on the other hand, are fantastic. As well as the usual – Star Wars figures, Lego – I've always had toy cars. One of my earliest memories of tricking out a vehicle of any kind involves a toy car my granddad gave me one Christmas. It was a Ford Capri. Only I wanted a cabriolet, so on Boxing Day I went into my dad's shed and tried to take the roof off with a Stanley knife. I did it eventually as well, but not before I nearly took my thumb off with a careless slip of the knife.

At first I'd gone at it with a pair of pliers and a screwdriver. I managed to crack the plastic glass of the back windscreen with the screwdriver and then bent the roof back with the pliers, but to get the roof off was going to require something a little more lethal. So I got out the

Stanley knife and started sawing away at the uprights on the back. I was sawing away, sawing away, sawing away and I sawed straight through the metal and into my thumb. When I went running into the house shouting 'Deep, deep, deep, deep, deep, deep!' and holding up my spouting hand to show my mum, my thumb was literally hanging off. It took seven stitches to put it back on. I can't remember what I told my mum I'd been doing. I don't think she cared: she was too busy worrying about the fact that my thumb was hanging off and my blood was going everywhere. My dad knew what I'd been doing though. He didn't say anything, but he knew. My dad's of the opinion that most parents can be too protective of kids. Instead of trying to stop me from doing dangerous things, my dad would say, 'He's going to hurt himself in a minute, watch this.' When I did, he'd turn round and say, 'Told you.' He always claimed it was the best way to learn, and, painful though the lessons were, he was usually right.

Remote control cars were the ultimate toy. I used to have remote control buggies and me and my mates would build race tracks and jumps for them and we'd drive them all over the farm. They were proper little all-terrain things and they could really go. They were toys, but they were quick little things. I never had Scalextric though. That was always too expensive. But it was okay because I used to save up and buy these remote control cars, a cross between a beach buggy and a stock car. They came in a kit that you'd build, and which I then used to modify – no surprise there. Like a junior remote control *Pimp My Ride* I'd sticker them up and paint the wheels and the rims, always trying to make them better. My mates never really used to bother tricking theirs out, so they were never quite as good as mine. Well, I didn't think so. My modifications didn't usually make them go any quicker, but they looked cooler.

The important thing, though – and this has really stuck with me – is that I always used to look after them well. Whereas most kids would use them and trash them, I would use them then maintain them and keep them in mint condition. Even now I can't stand it if something happens to one of my cars. If I kerb a wheel, that's it, it has to go straight off to have the wheels sorted out. These dings you get when some idiot in a Volvo opens his door on to yours; the little chips you get when gravel kicks up and nicks the paintwork – I can't stand to look at them. The second I spot something like that, that's it, it's got to be a respray straight away. I don't care how much it costs, I can't look at it. It's the one thing that really, really bugs me, and I was the same way about my cars even when they came with batteries and a little crystal radio control unit.

The other thing that's stuck with me since the days when I used to zoom my little tricked-out buggy around the hard standing out the back of our house is the ambition one day to have a proper track to race them on. When I was a kid, I used to dream of having a garden of my own. I decided that when I had my own house I was going to build a race track for my remote control cars, a proper track with little humps and jumps and everything. It was going to be ace. It never happened of course. You get older, you grow up, you pack away your childhood toys and your dreams change. Now I want a proper full-size track in my back garden. A proper tarmacked go-kart track to go all the way round the house and my back garden, for me and my mates to drive proper full-size go-karts around. I don't think the neighbours would be too happy, but it would be bloody cool.

4 THE CASTLE HOWARD RUBBISH RUN: THE FERRARI 308

My dad only ever had one great guiding philosophy in life: if you can walk, you can work. So if you wanted pocket money in our house, you bloody well worked for it. After a few years of odd-job earners, from mowing the lawn and other gardening tasks to helping out with the animals when my dad decided to 'have a go at farming', I officially went on the payroll at seven years old.

My first regular job was parking cars at Castle Howard. Not literally, of course – my feet wouldn't have reached the pedals and I'd never have got insurance. No, my job was directing cars into the car park when there were big events on at the house. There were a lot of weddings and corporate dinners there, when the likes of BP and Shell would pay loads to hire the place for a night and have big fireworks displays and military bands and that kind of thing. It was my dad's job to organise it all, including the parking. Castle Howard was the only place to work for miles around, especially if you were seven, so my dad put a word in and got me and my best mate David Coates the gig.

It was a big responsibility. On average there'd be something like three hundred people coming to an event, down the long driveway in coaches and cars, and you had to make absolutely certain that they parked in the right place or Simon Howard and the rest of the family who still own and run the house would get really upset. You had to make sure that all the visitors and guests parked on the right-hand side of the drive, not the left, because the left side was the Howard family's garden and they weren't too keen on people parking on it. Funny that. So I'd be there, with Herbert Press the gardener, who used to do all the edgings on the lawns and the flower beds and had done for something like 80 years. Herbert would go out in his flat cap, stop the traffic and direct the cars to the bottom of the drive where I'd get them to swing out to the left, and then I'd guide them as they backed up towards the fence on the right.

Because of the nature of the events, we used to get all kinds of amazing cars there. I'd be there helping Bentleys, Ferraris and Aston Martins to back up into spaces: to me, to me, bit more, bit more, stop. That's a lot of pressure for a seven-year-old. Obviously, once they were all parked and everyone was inside eating their lavish meals, we'd be out there, me and David, wandering around, looking at all these fantastic motors. We'd be there for hours, checking out all the angles, peering in through the windows, admiring bodywork; we'd be wowing over the big chrome bumpers on the Bentleys, the beautiful leather of the Astons and the exciting lines of the Ferraris. There'd be an event – a dinner, a concert or a wedding – every couple of weeks at least, sometimes more, and always there'd be these unbelievable motors.

It was like stepping into another world for me. My dad might have been the Don when it came to running Castle Howard, but he never earned big bucks. There was no Aston Martin or Mercedes or Bentley parked outside our house.

In fact the Howards themselves were never that big into cars, certainly not cool ones. They always preferred the reliable and the practical over the glamorous and the exciting, with the possible exception of Nick Howard, one of the sons, who, I would later discover, had better taste than anyone knew. (At least I think it was Nick, I never found out for certain.)

So parking those cars was a great job. David and I would have to be there for the whole evening because we had to see them out of the car park again at the end of the night, so we'd be there a good six hours, and we got paid quite well for it, something like a fiver a night, which for a seven-year-old was good money back then. You could buy quite a lot of Floral gums with that. Save it up long enough, which I of course did, and you'd have a new skateboard, or at least some new wheels and ball bearings to trick it out with. Either that or I'd buy something to do with motoring: a toy car, a model car, a remote control car, always something good. Not like most of my mates who, as soon as they got any spare cash, would do what my sister did and be straight off down the pound shop, blowing it on loads of rubbish they didn't really want. I always knew exactly what I wanted and I'd save every penny until I had enough to get it. That was my dad's logic. Even if he'd had the money he probably still wouldn't have given it to you because he wouldn't have thought you would appreciate it. Harsh but probably true, and definitely a good thing. Certainly none of the money I earned, from mowing my granddad's lawn to parking the cars at Castle Howard, was ever wasted.

By the age of nine David and I had been promoted to the pot wash. Well, it wasn't promotion so much as moving inside. It was still bloody cold though. The pot wash area was just outside the main kitchen. We didn't wash the pots from the kitchen itself, that was done by Izzy, a lovely old woman who was always bent over the sink. We used to wash all the cutlery and plates and glasses. As with the car park, we did this work when they were having big dinners and events at the house, but there was a cafeteria as well, which meant that we'd be working weekends too, making it a much more regular income than the car park gig. Saturday and Sunday I used to go up there and work, and after school as well, washing the cups and saucers in one of those industrial dishwashers, the ones where you pile everything up in a big wire basket, slide it into the machine, pull down the hood and a couple of minutes later all your plates come out clean and sparkling. It wasn't as exciting as seeing all those great cars but the money was good and there were plenty of opportunities for overtime.

At the end of the night David and I would have to take

the rubbish out. Now, having just catered for three hundred-odd people, the kitchens used to generate a hell of a lot of rubbish, and the bins were a hell of a long way away. It wasn't quite as simple as opening the kitchen door and sticking the black bin bags outside. Come the end of the evening there'd be a mountain of them piled up and they would need taking to the big industrial bins out by the garages right on the other side of the building. In the kitchen there were these tall trolleys designed to have metal trays slotted in them which were usually stacked with plates. Once we'd bagged all the rubbish, David and I would take those metal trays out, pile the trolleys high with black sacks and wheel them off. You could get about 16 black sacks on each trolley, and even then sometimes you'd need to do more than one journey.

Those trolleys used to make a hell of a racket, like a load of pots and pans being chucked down a staircase. You could hear us coming a mile off, which, given what lay ahead, was not a good thing. You'd take a run up the disabled ramp then go along this 150-foot-long corridor, past the toilets and through the door at the end, for which you needed a key. Once through that door you were into the back areas of Castle Howard. Imagine, it's a really old castle, all little archways and tiny dim lights. We're talking proper creepy. Not a place you really want to be late at night with nobody else around, or even with your best mate if he's just as freaked out as you are and who is making you even more jumpy.

What made it worse was that you knew somewhere out

there, down that corridor, waiting for you in the dark, behind a door that may or may not be locked (in our overactive imaginations it was always unlocked and open) was Tasha the dog. Tasha was this absolutely massive possessed dog that used to bark and snarl like it hadn't been fed in a decade. It was like a huge St Bernard Wolfhound cross and it used to frighten the shit out of everybody. If you listened really hard you could almost hear him sniffing you out as you stood there at the beginning of the corridor.

Needless to say, taking the rubbish to the bins was not something we looked forward to. You knew that if, God forbid, Tasha did actually get out he'd come screaming round the corner and rip you apart in ten seconds flat, no question. So we always had a plan of what we'd do, how we'd jink the trolleys and kink them this way so we'd be able to use them as a barricade before making a run for it. Ideally, though, you just wanted to get to the other end of the corridor as quickly and quietly as possible, and hopefully Tasha wouldn't hear you, or if he did you'd already be past his door (whichever one it was) and it would be too late for him to break it down, run out and claw you to shreds.

The corridor ran right under the Howards' private residence, so rubber matting had been put down to dampen the noise of the trolleys going backwards and forwards late at night. This was good. It at least gave us a fighting chance of making it past Tasha unheard. To up the odds even more in our favour, to make sure that the trolley didn't bounce and make a load of noise, and to ensure we got out of there as quickly as possible, as soon as we hit a straight stretch we used to jump on the trolleys and zoom down the corridor, jumping back off just before we hit the door at the end that led out into the courtyard area where the bins and garages were.

Normally that was the end of it. You'd unload all the bin bags, chuck them in the industrial bins, turn round and go back, praying to God that Tasha hadn't come to in the meantime. One night, though, something caught my eye. I've no idea how I saw it, it was just there in the corner of my eye, a flash of red paint through a crack in one of the garage doors. In that courtyard, just next to where the bins were, there were three big grey wooden garage doors. Usually what was behind them wasn't of much interest so I never bothered looking. The Howard family liked Land Rovers and Saabs and Volvos, which have to be the worst cars on the road not least because their drivers feel so safe in them they have absolutely no fear of taking everybody else out. But this one night the garage doors were open the tiniest bit, just a crack, and I could see this little bit of red paint.

I knew instantly what it was. I turned to David and shouted in a whisper, 'There's a fucking Ferrari in there!'

I told him to wait there, I was just going to have a look. I don't think David was upset about having to wait behind and stand guard, he was just shitting himself, giving me a look of terror that said, 'Don't do it, don't do it!'

I crept over to the door and pressed my eye to the gap – no harm in that. It was eleven pm and I was sneaking around the Howards' private garage when I should have been doing the bins – hardly a hanging offence. I was only there about five minutes, just looking through that crack, not doing any harm, but always looking back at David to make sure nobody was coming. He looked at me suddenly with an expression that said he knew exactly what I was thinking, and he started shaking his head. But it was too late. I'd pushed the door open.

I found myself inside the Howards' private garage looking at this stunning Ferrari. It was a 308GTB, with a hard top, but the fibreglass model. I knew this because I'd just given the bodywork a good tap. I may have been just nine years old but I knew my Ferrari 308GTBs from my 308GTSs (the soft-top) and I knew my fibreglass bodies from the later steel ones. I tapped on the body and looked at the deep spoiler at the front. Then I went round the side and ran my hand along the door panel and over the little black door latch. I gave it a little pull just to see what it did. And of course the door opened. I figured if I got caught at this point I was in deep shit anyway, and with the door open I was practically in the car already, so I thought, 'Sod it,' and I got in.

I just remember thinking, 'Bloody hell, I'm in a Ferrari. I'm in a Ferrari!' This was in the days of *Magnum*, when Tom Selleck used to drive a red 308GTS, so literally there was no cooler car on the planet. Remember, around that sort of time I was looking at my school mates' dads driving their Opal Mantas and thinking, 'Why can't my dad drive an Opal Manta?' That was about the size of it in my little village in North Yorkshire; but here I was sat in a Ferrari. Of course when you're a kid you have no idea about the worth of adult things like bricks and mortar, so to my nine-year-old car-obsessed mind this Ferrari was worth more than Castle Howard itself. It had to be at least a couple of hundred million quid surely, maybe even a trillion.

What I knew for a fact, though, was that I'd never sat in anything like it before. It had all these little toggle switches, a big chrome plate on the gated gearbox, black leather seats with these little studs on them (which they now call Daytona seating), a grey/black dashboard top, a black leather steering wheel with three metal spokes and the little prancing horse in the middle ... I just remember staring at that little horse, mesmerised by it. I was only in the car for four or five minutes, but it's like a photographic memory. I took in every single detail, drank it all in, absorbed it, convinced that I was never going to see another one as long as I lived, let alone sit in one (and if I hadn't I'd probably still have died happy knowing that I'd had the chance to experience one and taken it). This was my moment to see and remember everything about it.

And that's when I noticed it. The smell. That Ferrari smell. I'd never smelled anything like it ever, and the only time I've smelled it since is in other Ferraris. It's a special, Italian sports car, leather, luxury, money, petrol, passion kind of a smell, and it's unforgettable.

Nor will I forget the panic when I suddenly realised that of all the things I'd seen, not one of them was an interior door handle. I spent the next two minutes frantically searching for a way to get out (the door release on the 308 is extremely well hidden). Eventually I got the door open, and after rubbing my fingerprints off the paintwork I legged it back to David who was now looking more terrified than he'd ever looked at the thought of Tasha tearing him limb from limb.

That was the first time I sat in a Ferrari. As long as I live I'll be sure of one thing: I'll never forget that car. Every detail is still imprinted on my memory. As for who it belonged to, I never found out for sure. Of the two Howard brothers I always imagined it was Nick who was the proud owner of the 308GTB. Whoever it was, and whoever left that garage door open with the light on and the car unlocked, they made a young boy very, very happy – and later cost a grown-up chef a hell of a lot of money.

5 LES VOITURES (MERDE) DE MON PERE

I inherited many things from my father. My height, for one: I'm 6 ft 3 in and so was he when he was a strapping young lad. My work ethic: my father believed anything was possible if you were willing to work hard enough for it, a sentiment I wholeheartedly endorse. My temper: for both of us the line between calmness and absolute mayhem is a very fine one you don't really want to make us cross. And my love of food and wine: as well as being a catering manager my dad was an internationally respected sommelier, one of only two non-French judges on the Jurade de Saint Emilion, which classifies Bordeaux wines. Thankfully, though, of all the things I inherited from my father, his taste in cars wasn't one of them. If anything, the exact opposite is true. If he had a particular car, you can be pretty damn sure I never will. He has what can only be described as an unhealthy obsession with French cars. I, again thankfully, don't. The only thing he likes more than a French car is a cheap one. If it's French and cheap, well, nothing makes him happier.

My earliest motoring memories are of my dad's 'bargains'. Needless to say, they aren't happy memories. There was the MkI Escort, the Datsun Sunny, and the white Ford Capri 1.6 Laser with the brown cloth interior, the kind chocolate crumbs used to be drawn to and were then impossible to get off: when you tried scratching chocolate off the seats with your fingernail it just got even more attached and went white. Being a proper Yorkshireman, my dad could never resist a bargain. It didn't matter how rubbish the car he ended up with was, just as long as he got a good deal on it. I remember, years and years later, him ringing me up full of excitement and telling me that he'd just bought himself a Rolls-Royce. I thought, 'Bloody hell, this is it. He's done it. He's finally come to his senses. He's worked hard all his life, he's saved up his money and he's bought himself a proper Rolls-Royce.' I was genuinely excited for him and couldn't wait to see it. When I got to his house, there it was, sitting outside, his Rolls-Royce. And it was white. He'd gone and bought a white Rolls-Royce, like the ones they use for weddings – which was quite fitting really because he's on his third marriage. His liking for wedding cake and giving all his money away in divorce settlements are two more of his traits I managed to avoid, although my sister wasn't so lucky.

It's like he can't say no, to bargains or weddings. Yes, it's a hideous car and a horrible colour, and he probably knows it's a hideous car and he probably can't stand the colour either, but it's cheap, so he'll have it. If he had eight grand to spend on a car and there was a nice one he really liked for eight grand and one that was French and not very nice at all for six grand, he would buy the not-very-nice six grand one, even though he could afford the one he really wanted. If it was a bargain he just wouldn't be able to turn it down. I got my first car when I was twelve, a little Fiat 126, because someone offered it to him for £40. I'm not complaining. I loved that car, drove it all over the farm and had a great time in it. But I was twelve. I didn't need a car. All right, I'd had bikes and trikes and I'd driven tractors, and I know he thought it would be a good experience for me to learn to drive in the relative safety of the farm, but the reason he got it was because it had failed its MOT and someone at work was selling it cheap. It was a bargain too good to turn down. Same with the Beetle he bought my mum, and the six Minis he bought my sister. She wrote off five of them but he kept them coming because they were all cheap.

He was always getting a deal from some wheeler-dealer somewhere. Even his cars, which were partly for work and for which he had a budget, he had to try to get a deal on. He would never do what most of my mates do now, which is look at the 40 grand budget their work's given them for a car and think, 'If I add 20 grand of my own I can get something really good.' He would say, 'I've got 40 grand. If I can find a car for 20 grand I'll have saved 20 grand.' Which of course is what he did, and which was why all my mates' dads had amazingly cool cars and I was being dropped off at the school gates in a white Ford Capri 1.6 Laser with brown cloth interior.

It wasn't just cars my father's nose for a bargain got in

the way of. It also had a laughable effect on his 'farming' skills. As you already know, we weren't farmers, not really. My dad was a catering manager and my mum worked in a shoe shop – what did we know about farming? In his day job, my father was a very successful man; later, as promotions manager, he was responsible for bringing the filming of the the Granada TV version of *Brideshead Revisited* to Castle Howard and for putting on huge outdoor concerts featuring Bryan Ferry, José Carreras and Luciano Pavarotti. When he first started the place was attracting something like 30 or 40 visitors a day; when he left it was more like 4,000. Part of the deal was that the better you did at Castle Howard, the bigger the place you got, so we had a load of land with our house and it seemed a shame to waste it. As the place was called Lime Kiln Farm – the huge lime kiln was still there and perfect/lethal for a boy with a bike and no sense of danger – it was obvious to my dad that agriculture should be our sideline.

I think I was about five or six when my dad decided that it might be a good idea to try his hand at farming, and it was probably about eleven or twelve years later that my mother finally reached the end of her patience and decided that it wasn't. In between, I, along with the rest of my family, was subjected to a long list of ridiculous schemes. When we started breeding pigs, my dad spotted a 'bargain' boar in *Exchange & Mart* which was a deal too good to pass up, just like his cars. Now, anyone who knows anything about pig farming will tell you that in order to have good piglets you need good sows and, most importantly, a good boar. They'll also tell you that though boars can be very expensive, if you get a good one, it'll be an investment. My father had found a boar for sale for £50 – suspiciously cheap for most, but he thought it was his lucky day. He hitched the trailer up to the car, drove the 60 miles to Northampton, paid the old dear who was selling it, came back, put it in the pen next to the females – who were ready, able and by this time well up for it – opened the gate and waited. And waited. And waited. You've never seen a male so disinterested in the female of the species in your whole life. So my dad called the vet, who came over, took one look and asked, 'Where did you buy it from? It's not the one from Northampton is it?' Turned out this boar was famous as the only gay boar in the village. My dad went nuts. We were eating bacon for months after that.

My dad was just a useless farmer, there was no two ways about it. At one point we had 50 chickens, 25 cockerels and 25 hens, and the hens weren't laying. My dad, in his infinite wisdom, decided that the cockerels must be the problem, interfering with the hens and stopping them laying. So he went out one afternoon and just killed the cockerels. All of them. A week later, still nothing, no eggs, so he got the vet out again and it turned out that he'd got rid of the hens. We had 25 cockerels running around and my dad was waiting for them to lay.

In the end it was once again his complete inability to turn away a good deal that proved to be the last straw (pun intended). One day, for no reason other than it was really, really cheap, he decided to buy all the hay from the field next door. At the time we had pigs and cattle so we needed hay for feed and bedding. But we only had 16 pigs and a dozen cows and the field next door was bloody massive. A Texan ranch wouldn't have been able to use all the hay that came from it. When he had it delivered it made a 50 foot by 50 foot stack. As you drove up to the hill, you couldn't see the house any more, just this giant haystack. My mother was furious. It didn't help matters when she discovered that my dad had left all the windows open at the back of the house so there was hay and dust everywhere inside. That was it. My mother decided enough was enough, we were getting out of farming for good.

Meanwhile his fixation with cheap cars continued, and if it wasn't a bargain it had to be French. Peugeots, Citroëns, hideous, hideous things I had to go to school in which left me mentally scarred for life. After years of this cruel and unusual punishment I vowed never to buy a French car, and I never will. He had a Peugeot 306, a 406, a 505, Citroën Xantias, an XM and a BX, the one with the hydraulic suspension that made the back go up and down although no one ever really knew why. They were dreadful cars that looked like they'd been specifically designed to be rubbish. I can only think that his obsession with French cars was because he loved French food and wine. I listened to him on the subject of the food and the wine, but not the cars. They were crap. And I mean really crap.

My dad's apparent phobia of anything even approaching a proper driver's car is all the more ironic when you know that he's actually an ex-traffic copper. Not only that, he used to be an advanced police driving instructor. Yes, he actually taught policemen how to drive. When we were kids, if me and my sister were playing up in the back of the car and my mother wasn't around, he'd suddenly pull some of his old moves and scare the shit out of us. That would shut us up. Back when he was chasing robbers all over the south of England he used to drive a big MkII Jag, like the one Inspector Morse had, only with a blue light and a siren. Literally, you couldn't get anything further removed from a Citroën Xantia if you tried. I can only think that he felt he got all the driving he wanted to do out of his system when he was in the police force and didn't see the point of having something more driveable afterwards. Maybe it was enough for him to know he could do it; he didn't need a flash motor to prove it. Still, a MkII Jag to a BX?

Maybe it has something to do with how he left the police force. He's a real no-nonsense type of a character, my dad, not one for big shows of emotion or niceties. He's all about getting the job done and that's that, and he's got loads of great stories about giving yobs and nutters a bit of old-fashioned treatment, the kind where the rule book went out the window and the baddies got what was coming to them.

The best was always the one about the armed robbery in Pepworth in Brighton. The robbers escaped in a Transit van and were thought to be heading to London. Everyone knew that if they made it to the capital they'd get away, so the best chance the police had was to stop them en route. My dad was sat in his MkII Jag in a lay-by on the A3, listening to the reports coming in on his radio – details of the robbery, a description of the robbers and their van, which of them was armed, their current location – and he realised they were heading his way. After a while he saw them coming up the hill, and knowing that they had to be stopped before they got much closer to London he decided the only thing to do was throttle down and T-bone them. Which he did. He T-boned them so hard that he knocked their van off the road and into a ditch, and his MkII ended up on top (he said this was probably just as well because it meant they couldn't open the doors, and if they'd got out they would probably have shot him). It was a good result. When the chasing police cars arrived they nicked the robbers and everyone was happy. But in taking them off the road my dad had rolled his Jag and done his back in, and he had to leave the force as a result. He then did what all ex-coppers do: he ran a pub. Two very successful pubs in fact. Then he moved to York where he ran a Terry's restaurant (as in the people who make the chocolate oranges), which is where he met my mother, who was going out with Stan the head chef at the time. She dumped him for my dad, the restaurant manager. (Head Chef Dumped for Restaurant Manager – story of my life, that is.) From there he went to Castle Howard, and his interest in cars and driving has rarely been seen since. Which was a shame, because when you're a kid, getting a new car is the most exciting thing in the world. I can remember as clear as if it were yesterday the day my best mate David Coates's parents got their MkII Escort. Now that was a cool car. It was only 2 litre, but that didn't matter, it was just a really cool car. Even the 1.6, the RS, was cool. Some cars are just cool, and the one David Coates's parents had just bought definitely qualified. I can also clearly remember the day my dad got his new Citroën XM, and we arrived at school just as another good mate of mine was pulling up in his dad's brand-new bright red Opal Manta (which, as I said, is quite obviously shit now but back then was the bollocks).

Ten years old, my dad's got a brand-new car, I arrive at school, and the whole car park, David's MkII Escort and the Manta included, just Top Trumps me.

Even when my dad did come close to getting it right he still managed to find the world's most uncool cars. I don't know what happened. I think he must have been hit on the head one day, but he suddenly went from buying nothing but French cars to nothing but Audis. Ordinarily this would have been a very good move, but once again my dad's love of a bargain did its worst. First we had an Audi 80, in gold, which he got because it was cheap. Of course it was cheap. Who the hell wants to drive a gold car? After that we moved up in the world with an Audi 100. A metallic lime green one. With a lime green interior. Jesus Christ you were buzzing when you got to school if you got a lift in that. No wonder I always preferred to ride my bike the 5 miles to school rather than face the embarrassment (and the headache).

The only time I can ever remember being genuinely excited at the thought of my dad buying a new car was one afternoon in York at the end of a long day touring the showrooms as part of our ritual two-yearly car hunt. For some reason it was just me and my dad going round the usual suspects, looking at the least exciting cars you could ever imagine – well, he was; I was looking at the latest hot hatches. After going to all the Peugeot and Citroën garages he knew, we made an unexpected stop at a very different type of showroom. I knew the garage in question well because I used to pass by it when I walked my gran's Yorkshire terrier Tuppence. It always had a very fine selection of the latest sports cars on display. Not the kind of place you'd expect to find my father.

We went in, and sandwiched between a white and green Lotus Cortina and a white Ford Escort RS Turbo was a red Lotus Eclat with cream interior. Definitely not my father's kind of car. My dad was, as always, in a suit, so the sales-man was all over him like a rash, and before I knew what was happening he was handing the keys to my dad who looked at me, winked, and asked me if I fancied a spin. My dad wanted to go for a spin, in a Lotus Eclat. I couldn't believe it. I really, really couldn't believe it. I wasn't just surprised, I was in shock.

Off we went down the road in the red Lotus Eclat with the cream leather and suddenly my dad came alive. Speed-ing down the dual carriageway it was like he was back in his MkII Jag, chasing bad guys and showing what a former advanced police driving instructor could do. It was like the car had instantly taken 20 years off him.

He didn't buy it of course. It wasn't French, it certainly wasn't a bargain, and no doubt my mother would have had more than a few things to say about it. I was a little disappointed when he handed the keys back, but at the same time I was so shocked by the fact that we'd gone out in it in the first place I don't think I ever got as far as thinking about what might happen at the end of the test drive. It's a shame really. For a minute there he looked like he was really enjoying himself, like he'd remembered there was more to cars than deals and boot space. I wish he'd rediscover it again, blow off the cobwebs and the stink of garlic and get behind the wheel of a proper car. It'll never happen though. Last I heard he'd just bought a Citroën Xantia. The cheap one.

6 BMXs, BUNNY-HOPS AND BROWNIES

It's 1983, I'm ten, I've got a regular job washing pots in the kitchens of Castle Howard, and I've just got a Raleigh Aero-Pro Burner. Life doesn't get much better.

You see, the Raleigh Aero-Pro Burner wasn't just a BMX, it was the coolest BMX there was. Chrome frame, black five-spoke mag wheels, black pads, it was a proper BMXer's bike – or it was when I was finished with it – and I was a proper BMXer. For me, BMXing was the realisation of my skateboarding dream. I could never really do skateboarding. I had all the gear, I'd tricked my board out and I was ready to pull some moves – ride railings, flip my board, fly off half pipes – but I just couldn't stand up on the thing. BMXing was much more my thing. I was a natural.

I could do allsorts on my Aero-Pro Burner, especially once I'd tricked it. I put pegs on the front and back, like extended wheel nuts that you'd stand on to do tricks; I used them to do front bunny-hops and rear bunny-hops. I could also do front and rear bunny-hops on the pedals – much harder than on the pegs. I used to do the thing where you'd drive along, hit the front brakes so the rear end would go up, and you'd flick it round and on to something like a bench; if you had enough momentum you could bring the front up as well so the whole bike was on the bench; then you could do some bunny-hops on the pedals and jump back off again. I could even do the move where you applied the front brake, kicked the back end round and literally stepped over the frame as it swung round you. That was pretty cool. I could do loads of other things too – pick it up off the floor just by standing on the pedal, wheelies, all the usual stuff – but those were my coolest moves. I used to change the hand grips, which were a bit of a bugger to do because you had to use a scalpel to get the old ones off (and with my track record for blade injuries that was asking for trouble), then to get the new ones on you had to slide them on with Fairy Liquid, and then you had to wait for them to dry and set otherwise they'd forever be twisting round. I used to change the forks and the handlebars as well, anything to make the bike cooler and better for stunts.

I was obsessed with that bike; it completely changed my world. Before that I'd had a Raleigh Boxer, which was like a baby BMX. Mine was yellow, so it was sort of cool, but my neighbours had a Chopper and a Grifter, and next to those it was a case of little man/big man syndrome ('How big is yours?'). My piddly little Boxer was, well, little. I couldn't actually ride Grifters because they were too big for me. I couldn't reach the floor. But I borrowed my neighbour's Chopper once and that was really cool – or it was until I came off, and because my legs weren't long enough to touch the ground properly I ripped my bollocks on the gear stick. That really bloody hurt.

Once I had the Aero-Pro Burner, though, it was a different story. I was the man, I was unstoppable. When I got that bike I suddenly got my freedom.

I rode absolutely everywhere on it. I used to bike the 5 miles to school every day, and that's a lot of pedalling. Me and David Coates, who had an Xtra Burner which was all right but not as good as mine, used to ride out to this old campsite, next to the lake at Castle Howard. We'd do a circuit of the campsite and the guy who ran it always used to come out and shout and tell us off, but we didn't care. We'd fly past and ignore him. One day he put a scaffolding bar across the top of the gate posts. We didn't see it until it was too late. We were lucky it didn't take our heads off. It was like some comedy sketch: one minute we were bombing along, standing on our pedals, the next we were swinging from a metal bar and our bikes were hurtling off into the distance without us. We could hardly breathe we were so winded. I'm not sure we went back there after that. But there were plenty of other places for two BMXers to get into trouble. Plenty.

The first time I got arrested I was on my Aero-Pro Burner. There was this disused farmhouse about 4 miles away from the back of our farm; no one had lived in it for ten years at least. One day David and I decided to ride over there. It was completely abandoned, like something out of *Scooby Doo*, so of course we climbed in through a window and found all this amazing stuff, like tankards, and playing cards with half-naked women on them. We thought, 'Right, we're having them,' so we loaded them up and took them back to our den.

Our den was round the back of the farm. It was almost like a hayloft, with a rope ladder we used to get up to it. It looked really cool with all the loot from the old farmhouse in it. Then one day my dad found it. He realised what we'd done and he did what any reasonable protective father would do: he called the police. They came and took me away and put me in a cell. I was ten. There was no mention of David, it was just me, on my own, down the local nick. No one had been in this farm for a decade, it's not like anyone was going to miss anything, but my dad wanted to teach me a lesson, and being an ex-copper he was mates with the local police, so they banged me up and left me in a cell for two hours. I got hauled in front of the super-intendent and everything. Got a right ear bashing. It was almost as if my dad had orchestrated it all and told them exactly what to say. And it was all staged, but I was ten years old. I thought I was going down.

We never went back to the old farmhouse. Instead we found other ways to amuse ourselves, one of which involved a ramp and the local girls' Brownie pack. I had this BMX ramp, a really, really good one, that I'd bought with my pocket money. It was 3 feet long with a strip of that non-slip black sandpaper type stuff up the centre for extra grip, and it had clips at the back so you could set it to different heights. We used to set it up in David's back garden, or at the bottom of the hill on the farm. We'd both pedal furiously down the hill towards it, picking up a fair speed to the point where we couldn't actually pedal as fast as we were going, we'd go flying off the end of this thing, and we'd go a pretty long way. Our other place to jump was outside the village hall. There wasn't a hill to ride down, but there was a mound of grass by the car park which was perfect for giving the ramp extra height, so what you lost in run-up speed you made up for in launch angle.

Usually when we were trying to outjump each other we'd mark the distance with a stick. One of us would jump, the other would record the distance with the stick, then we'd swap. We could do that for hours. One day we were outside the village hall with our ramp when the local Brownies, who used to meet in the village hall, turned up. There they all were, gathering in the car park in their nasty brown dresses, yellow scarves and woggles, and there we were, jumping off our ramp and measuring the results with a stick. All of a sudden someone – and to be fair, I think it was one of the Brownies – came up with a great idea.

'Why don't we lie down, and you can jump us.'

Brilliant!

I reckoned I could jump 15 feet off this thing, which when you're only 3 feet tall is a bloody long way, but I had no idea how many Brownies that would be, so we started off with two.

When the two Brownies were in place, we took as long a ride up as possible, pedalled furiously, went up the ramp and over. No problem. We put a third Brownie down, took a run up, pedalled furiously, got over, no problem. A fourth, a fifth and a sixth were added, and by the time we reached Brownie number 13 we were worn out from all the pedalling. We didn't want to risk chopping a 14th Brownie in half so we put my sister's big ted on the ground instead. We made it, just about, and then decided it was probably best to quit while we were ahead.

So that was it, the height of my BMXing achievements and my first real experience of women and some of their very strange ideas, all in one aerobatic stunt-riding go. Magic. What can I say? It was a small village in the middle of nowhere. We had to make our own entertainment.

7 BIKES AND TRIKES

The lime kiln at the far end of Lime Kiln Farm was this huge great mound, about 30 feet high, like a mini volcano, hollow inside with a big opening at the top. If you had a little motorbike (which I did), and you were a small kid (which I was) who had no fear (which I didn't), it was perfect for riding your motorbike round the top of, daring yourself to get closer and closer to the edge, being careful not to get too close or you'd drop right into it, and it was a long way down. If I wasn't jumping Brownies on my BMX or being thrown in a police cell for nicking playing cards with naked women on them, this is how I used to amuse myself.

I was about eleven when I got my first motorbike, a little Puch 50 twist-and-go scrambler. I went with my dad to Makro the discount supermarket one day when he was buying a load of drink for work, and this little bike was just waiting there. It was white with red and blue stripes and a sticker with PUCH written on it on the fuel tank. I gave it a proper look over. I sat on it and fiddled with all the bits and pieces. My dad was watching me, and after a while, once he'd got all the things he was there for, he just picked up a boxed one – it was only a little thing – and put it in his trolley. I asked him what he was doing, and he said, 'You like it? You can have it. But you'll pay for half of it.' It was £150, and the maximum I'd earned that year was £40, so I had to come up with £75. Sure enough I worked to pay for it, pot washing like crazy, and the money went straight to my dad because he knew that if I got hold of the money he'd never see it. He wasn't stupid.

I used to ride all over the fields on that thing. Either on my own or with my mate Philip Schofield. No, not that Philip Schofield. This Philip Schofield lived about 3 miles away and had an XT175, a massive bike for him and far too big for me, a big black thing with a black and white tank. Either I would cane it over to his and bomb around his fields, or he would come over to mine and we'd bomb around by the kiln. We had to stick to the fields though. I wasn't allowed to ride out on the road on the Puch 50; for that I had my BMX. Even though we weren't out on the roads, I always used to wear a crash helmet because I used to come off a lot, and of course the more confident you get, the more you come off, and I was always pretty confident on my little Puch 50. There wasn't anywhere I wouldn't go, and that included up the side of the kiln.

Because I was only small and the little Puch 50 was pretty light, if I had a good run at it I could usually get up the side of the kiln. But it was steep, and the inside was even steeper. You could drive up the outside, but you couldn't then drive down into the hole and back up the other side to the top again because it was way too steep, practically a vertical drop when you looked down into it from the top. It was so steep that the inside would have made an almost perfect wall of death to ride round, if it hadn't been for the big hole in the front, which was presumably where they used to put things into the kiln. Shame, that would have been amazing to ride round. It's probably just as well though. The place was lethal enough as it was.

I took incredible care of my little Puch. I had it for about a year, and when I wasn't testing my skills to the limit I was cleaning and polishing and taking good care of my pride and joy. Until one day it was nicked. I was gutted. It wasn't insured or anything. My dad always said to me, 'When you're finished with it, lock it up and put it in the shed and then lock the shed to be on the safe side.' And, like an idiot, I didn't. One night I left it on the hard standing at the back of our house and it got stolen. I woke up in the morning and it was gone. I was heartbroken. I went in tears to my dad, who in typical style said, 'You'll learn, that'll teach you.' He didn't say, 'Don't worry, I'll get you another one,' it was always, 'You'll learn.' About three days later it turned up at the bottom of the village next to the telephone box. It had been completely stripped, all the leads had been pulled off it, and it had been set alight. It was just a burnt-out pile of bits, completely wrecked. I think the sight of that was worse than having it nicked in the first place. I loved that bike so much.

So that was that. My Puch 50 was no more. I was back to

my BMX and working hard to save money to buy another motorbike.

Once I'd got a bit of cash together I went with my dad to the bike shop to look for a replacement. I was looking around at the Puch 50s, Yamahas and Hondas, and in the corner sat this shiny, brand spanking new Honda ATV70 three-wheeler. Now, these things really were lethal. No one knew that at the time, of course, but they ended up being replaced by quad bikes because they were so dangerous. It looked great in the shop and I said to my dad, 'I like that.' I only had about half the money though – my savings plus Christmas and birthday presents. I sat on it and thought it was really cool, but knowing that there was no way I could afford it I got off, had another look round and pointed out another small motorbike, nowhere near as nice as the trike but nowhere near as expensive either. I said to my dad, reluctantly, 'I'll have that one.' My dad looked the little motorbike over, nodded and said, 'Right, I'll pay, you go and wait in the car.' So I gave him my money and went and sat in the car.

Next thing I knew the door of the shop was opened and my dad was wheeling out the big Honda trike and pushing it into our horse box. I couldn't believe it. I guess he must have liked it as much as I did.

We got home and filled it with fuel. My dad informed me that this was a serious bit of kit and that we were going to have to read the instructions. Then he was going to show me how to ride it. Like he knew how to ride it. I don't think he'd ever seen one before, never mind driven one. But there he was, on the courtyard round the back of the house, looking it over like you do when you're buying a new car, consulting the instructions and telling me that it had three gears, that's the throttle, that's the brake ...

'Right,' he said when he'd finished his piece, 'are you watching? I'm going to show you how to use it.'

He started it up with the pull cord (like the one you get on a lawn mower), sat on it, revved it up and put it into first gear. Only he still had the throttle on, and as soon as he released the clutch that was it, it reared up and fell straight back on top of him. He's lying on his back in the middle of the courtyard pinned to the ground by this trike and I'm pissing myself laughing. And there ended my very first trike lesson. Still, there was an important lesson there for me, which inevitably I didn't learn.

Blatting it up the side of the old lime kiln was easy enough on my little Puch 50, but on the Honda ATV70 it was a different story altogether. Looking at the stupidly steep side of the kiln now, it's obvious it was never going to happen. When you're a kid, though, you think that because you got up there on your little 50cc bike it should be no problem for this big three-wheeler, just as long as you get a good run at it.

Before long I was bombing it up there. The further up the mound you went, the steeper the gradient got and the more you needed to lean over the front to stop the bike rearing up; only the more you lean over the front, the less traction the back wheels have, and the steeper the gradient, the more traction you need. By the time I was three-quarters of the way up the side of the kiln I was on a 60 degree slope, leaning right over the front, and the rear wheels started to spin. And before I could say, 'Oh fuck, what do I do?' I found myself rolling slowly backwards wishing I'd stayed indoors and played Connect Four with my sister, like she'd asked. I was rolling, rolling, rolling, then suddenly it reared up and fell straight back, literally right on top of me.

Unlike my dad, however, I wasn't flat on my back in the courtyard, I was upside down halfway up a steep hill with the trike not only on top of me but dug in. I was pinned down and I couldn't move the thing, the angle of the slope making the trike even heavier and harder to budge. I started to panic, not least because I could smell petrol. Really, really strongly. And the engine was still running. I thought it could just be petrol coming out of the breather pipes, which isn't such a big deal, but when I looked down to check I saw fuel pouring straight out of the tank. The petrol cap, which I was straddling, upside down, was leaking and the fluid was going all over my jeans. We're talking about two Coke cans' worth, all over my crotch.

I managed to turn the engine off, but I still couldn't move it left or right. After several efforts I finally shifted it just enough to be able to drag myself out from under it. Without me underneath it, the trike destabilised, rolled over and then slid off down the hill, but I didn't give a toss about it by this point because the petrol had soaked right through to my skin and was now burning me in the worst possible place. The pain was pain like you've never felt in your life. It was literally like having my bollocks marinated in battery acid. It fucking hurt. There was nothing for it, the jeans had to come off. It hurt so much that I took my pants off too.

I then ran down the hill, shouting, screaming and wailing, with nothing on below the waist, not a stitch, swinging my tackle in an effort to cool myself down, and across the field, straight past a family of ramblers in cagoules. God knows what they thought, but I wasn't stopping to find out. When I reached the outside tap in the courtyard I turned it on and literally stood there under the water, like someone who'd been in the desert for a month and needed a drink. I just sat there with cold water running all over my little todger. No lasting damage was done, you'll be pleased to know, but I dread to imagine what would have happened if I'd been under that trike much longer.

I never told anyone about my manhood's close call. The trike was still in one piece so no one needed to know. If she'd found out, my mother would probably have stopped me going on the trike altogether. My dad, on the other hand, would probably have argued with her that at least I was learning lessons. Where my mother always wanted to protect, my dad was all for character building.

Sometimes I could see his logic, other times it just seemed cruel. I was always one of the quiet kids at school and was horrendously bullied for it. I used to get the shit kicked out of me all the time. At lunch I'd always get a good kicking, maybe have snow rubbed in my face if it was winter. I'd come home and my jacket would be ripped and I'd be covered in bruises. It got to the point where my mother was desperate to pull me out of school but my father wouldn't hear of it. 'No,' he used to say, 'he'll stand on his own two feet and he'll fight it. No son of mine's going to run away. Let him face it.' It's a fine line between character building and character crushing, a very fine line.

My mother always wanted to keep me on the safe side of that line. Which is why I think she let me have the bikes in the first place, even though I couldn't ride them on the road. I think she felt it was better that I got it out of my system in the relative safety of the farm rather than rush out at 16 and go crazy on the road. And she was right. When I was 16 I lost two very good friends in bike accidents. Neither had had motorbikes before. They turned 16, got a bike each, and were dead within twelve months.

Still, my mother would have been horrified if she'd known some of the things me and my mates got up to, especially on that Honda trike.

At the back of our house there was a hedge with gaps in it, and for some reason we thought it would be a really good idea to get my air rifle and try to shoot each other through the gaps as we rode past on the trike. One of us would be in the field with the air rifle, another would be on the trike on the other side of the hedge, riding backwards and forwards, being shot at. We were all rubbish shots and never managed to hit the rider, so really we just spent hours and hours riding up and down in a straight line and missing our target. I don't know why, but me and my mates thought this was great fun. I know, I know, it's not big and it's not clever, and I'm not suggesting for a moment that it was a good idea. Kids, if you're reading this, don't do it. But it used to keep us out of Mum's hair for hours. We were farmers' kids, that's what farmers' kids do. Well, it's what we did. Things are different in the country. It's not like kids growing up in the city. We didn't talk weird and play with knives – well, you know what I mean. Most importantly, though, no one ever got hurt when we were out and about. Not unless you count a few petrol burns in private places.

And the time we ran over Philip Schofield in my Fiat 126.

8 PHILIP SCHOFIELD IS DEFINITELY NOT A CHICKEN: THE FIAT 126

My first experience of driving on four wheels came on a tractor. My dad had a big old Ferguson and he used to put me on his knee and let me steer; he would do the gears and the pedals. I was about eight at the time so my feet couldn't reach. When I was ten I started driving it for real. It was a massive old thing and the steering was really heavy so I couldn't drive it very far because it was such hard work. I'd drive it around the farm, but no more than maybe 400 yards before turning it round and coming back again. It was a proper old-fashioned model, with the tall exhaust pipe on the front, a flap on the top and tons of smoke belching out. Point is, by the time I got my first car, a little Fiat 126, at the age of twelve, I was already a pretty experienced motorist.

My dad figured that buying that car was cheaper than driving lessons, and he was right. He bought it off one of the staff at work for £40. It was completely knackered, they just wanted to get rid of it, and always being one for a bargain my dad jumped at it. It really was unfit for the roads, but it was great for whizzing around the farm. And because we lived in the middle of nowhere, my dad was always looking for ways to keep us, or more specifically me, entertained. After bikes and trikes, a car was the natural progression. (Well, it was either that or get a bigger bike, and the only thing to get after a Honda ATV70 trike would have been a Suzuki scrambler, which were quick little things – they'd do 90 miles an hour easy – and bound to get me into exactly the kind of trouble he was hoping to avoid.) He thought that if he didn't focus my attention on an exciting piece of machinery I was going to go off and do all the stuff the other kids did, like, say, nicking things from empty farmhouses, being led astray by girls in uniforms, and messing about with air rifles. All the things I wouldn't dream of doing. Never. Not me. Getting me a cheap banger was by far the safest option. More fool him.

The 126 was a tiny thing, just a bit bigger than the classic Fiat 500s, which I still love (I've actually got an original Abarth race model at home). It was dark blue with brown cloth interior – my childhood seems to have been cursed with brown cloth interiors – and it had a manual five-speed gearbox, no radio and a heater you couldn't use because it reeked of something toxic, probably exhaust fumes, which made your eyes burn every time you turned it on. It was great. My dad taught me how to drive it in the courtyard round the back of the house, this time more successfully than his trike masterclass, and within minutes I was tearing around the fields. That thing provided me with hours and hours of fun.

And of course, once I'd mastered the five-speed gearbox, the clutch and driving in tractor ruts, all I needed to do was make it my own with a little customisation. So out came the masking tape and a couple of cans of yellow and red spray paint from Halfords and before you could say 'pimp my ride' my dark blue Fiat 126 had an unbelievably cool set of red and yellow flames coming off the front wheel arches and all the way down the side. Then, instead of a glass windscreen, it had chicken wire, which along with the blacked-out side windows (which you couldn't actually see out of because I'd painted them with black spray paint – smart move) made it look like a proper rally car.

At least that was the official reason I gave for why the car suddenly had a chicken wire windscreen. The truth has been a closely guarded secret until now. My Fiat 126's windscreen lost its glass when we ran over Philip Schofield (no, not that Philip Schofield!) in a game of chicken.

The rules of the game were simple, the same as all the hundreds of other games of chicken we'd played on our motorbikes and trikes over the years, the same as every game of chicken ever. One person stands in the middle of a field (in this case Philip) while someone else (in this case me and the rest of our mates in the car) drives at them. The person who bottles it and moves first is the chicken. Philip didn't move. I've no idea why not, he just didn't. There were four of us whizzing across that field in the Fiat, really hoofing it, doing a good 30 miles an hour. We were all looking at him, waiting for him to jump out of the way, and he was looking at us, waiting for us to swerve. We were looking at him and he was looking at us and the next thing, BANG!, we hit him. He hit the windscreen and went straight over the top. The 126 had a cloth sunroof which was open at the time, and I swear we all watched in horror as poor Philip flew over our heads. I remember his legs appeared to go past in slow motion. I looked in the rear-view mirror to see if I could see him, more importantly to see if I could see him moving. Everyone else in the car was shouting, 'You've killed him, you've killed him!' I did a handbrake turn and spun the car round just as Philip was getting up. I couldn't believe it. Not only was he alive, he was in one piece. I seriously thought I'd ended his life.

The new priority suddenly became keeping him quiet. I couldn't afford to have my mother finding out or that would have been it, we wouldn't have had the car any more. In the end I made a pact with Philip. I told him that if he didn't tell anyone we'd run him over I'd let him drive the car when he came round, which was a pretty big deal because I wouldn't let anyone drive my car, so it seemed like fair compensation for running him over. Philip agreed and became the only person I ever allowed to drive that Fiat 126, although he could only drive it at certain times and in certain places as I didn't want my mum or dad to see him at the wheel because they would have known straight away that something wasn't quite right.

The windscreen wasn't quite as easy to fix. The glass had cracked side to side where he'd hit it. One look at that and my mum would have wanted to know what we'd been up to, so I kicked the windscreen out, got some chicken wire from the farm and added 'rally windows' to my list of modifications.

Even after that, and with no windscreen, I used to drive that car like a lunatic over the fields. Just over the fields though, nowhere else. It was brilliant.

Not long after that my dad started taking me to Tockwith Aerodrome to teach me to drive properly. Tockwith was a disused old airfield near where we lived where parents would take their kids to learn the basics before going out on the road. It cost something like a fiver a go and you could drive round there all afternoon. Fittingly it's now an approved go-karting school. Everyone else learning there was 17 or 18; I was there with my dad teaching me to mirror, signal, manoeuvre when I was 13.

We used to go over there in his Audi. We'd swap seats and he'd be straight back in advanced police driving instructor mode, telling me how to do it properly, and I mean properly. It wasn't just all about the three-point turns and the reverse parking. He taught me to anticipate, to control my speed and brake with the gears, to go side-ways, the lot. He must have been doing something right because I passed my test first time after only one hour-long lesson. I had intended to have more lessons, but I applied for my test as soon as I got my provisional licence; I had after all already been driving for five years by then. I got someone else's cancellation, so one lesson immediately before my test was all there was time for. I turned 17 on 30 June and I passed my test on 7 July. So you see, my dad was right: at £40 my little Fiat 126 really was cheaper than driving lessons.

I'm not sure Philip Schofield was ever quite the same after his brush with the Fiat though.

9 *FRANCE IN AN HGV*

When it comes to education, I'd say some of the most important things I learnt came from going on trips to France with Dad in his HGV. My dad has spent his life being a jack of all trades, and he's actually been very good at some of them. He was not only a renowned sommelier and judge on the Jurade de Saint Emilion, he was also one of the two main UK importers of wine from the Bordeaux region. Always keen to save a couple of quid, he didn't just import the wine, he got his HGV licence, hired a lorry and went to collect it himself. And I used to go with him.

I was never good at school. I even failed cookery. I was always just too thick to be academic. My sister was the one with the brains and I was more practical. If it involved anything written I wouldn't be able to do it, which was one of the reasons I failed cookery, or 'home economy' as it was called then. I say one of the reasons; I'm convinced the other was that the home economy teacher hated me because I could cook better than she could. I think everyone just assumed I wasn't putting any effort into my written work, but that wasn't true. I'd sit there for hours, night after night, trying to write up how to cook an angel cake, or put into words the concept for a new design of kitchen cupboard, and I'd always get a D for it.

Actually, look at my school books, and the diagrams and illustrations that went with the writing were always incredibly detailed and painstaking, which should have given someone a clue that I was putting more than a D's worth of effort in. In truth, those drawings took half the time it took me to do the writing yet would easily get me an A. If not the quality of those drawings, then the effort I put into practical work was surely enough to make anyone who was half awake realise that I had a genuine passion for the subject which my writing wasn't reflecting, and that maybe there was something more fundamental wrong. But my teacher was too busy filling my exercise books with must-try-harders to notice that it was only the words that were the problem.

As for English, I didn't even try to concentrate on it. What was the point? Shakespeare, Dickens – what good were they to me? My brain just switched off to anything printed that wasn't in a car magazine. Put me in art or cookery, doing something creative or practical, and I came alive; get me to read out loud, and I was like the slow kid in the class. It wasn't until much later, when I first had to read an autocue for *Saturday Kitchen*, that someone worked out I wasn't the thick kid after all, I was in fact dyslexic.

I was 13 when we first went over to the South of France

together to collect the wine. It was a week-long round trip: two days there, two days back, and the rest of the time he'd leave me in a French chateau to learn what French food was really all about. Through Castle Howard and his connections with Saint Emilion he knew the families who ran these great old chateaux and they were more than happy to have a young wide-eyed wannabe chef stay for a few days. Every visit was to somewhere different, but every time it was just as incredible and eye-opening. You couldn't imagine a greater culture shock if you tried. I was growing up in England at a time when a Berni Inn was considered an exotic place to eat. If it didn't come with chips and an all-you-can-eat salad bar it was completely alien. All of a sudden I was being dropped off at these big family houses where some of the greatest chefs in the world had trained and I was being looked after by the lady of the house who had in her head the entire history of French cooking.

These were some of the best chateaux in France – Figeac, Pressac, Cheval Blanc – so I was meeting real experts, the people who actually trained the chefs. It wasn't restaurant food, it was authentic rustic French cooking, the foundations and building blocks of every great French restaurant. It was proper French food, at its very best, and I was in there, taking it all in, while my dad was off in Saint Emilion sorting out his HGV-load of wine.

This was my first experience of good wine and food (there was no such thing as shit wine or food out there). And it was my first experience of proper French food: foie gras, truffles and pigeon – not just pigeon breasts, but pigeon, with the head still on. It was also my first real experience of markets. At home, if you had to go food shopping it was off down to Sainsbury's. Here, the cook would take me to the local market, point at a quacking duck in a cage and say, 'Canard.' And I'd be going, 'Yeah, yeah, duck.' The next thing, the duck would have had its neck wrung and it'd be lying in her shopping basket. They didn't do that at Sainsbury's. We'd pluck it, dress it, keep the head on, and while the duck was in the oven the cook would pan-fry the liver and spread it on a piece of toast for me. And there was no 'I don't fancy it'. You were eating it, and that was that. Put it this way: it made for a very sharp culinary learning curve.

I learned so much so quickly in those kitchens, but if there's one thing I learned quicker than anything else it was that the secrets to great cooking are fantastic ingredients and passion. For the French, cooking is all about going to the market, spending time looking around, picking out the freshest meats and vegetables, something which as a young boy from England I just wasn't used to. In these villages they didn't have a local supermarket, they had stalls in a square with absolutely everything you could ever want on them. It was amazingly exciting – the colours, the smells, the noise of the animals. It was an eye-opener, but a great one.

I went back year after year, at first with my dad on the wine runs in the HGV, then when I was at catering college on six-week blocks of work experience. I was cooking in two-star Michelin kitchens in my teens, and my head spun with it all. It was all light years ahead of anything we learned in school (or even catering college), and being 15 and versed in the ways of true French culinary excellence didn't always go down so well. In fact, one time it almost got me expelled.

One day our teacher informed us that the following week we could cook whatever we wanted. So a few days later all the girls – and there were 24 girls in my cookery class at school, and three boys, which was probably what attracted me to it in the first place – brought in the ingredients for Black Forest gateau, Swiss roll, nut cutlets and angel cakes with buttercream. I brought in what I needed to make chicken livers flambéed in brandy with a mange tout and rocket salad. Amazingly, the teacher was not impressed. I was in the corner, flambéing away, when she suddenly shouted out, 'James! What do you think you're doing?' I said, 'Er, flambéed chicken livers with a mange tout and rocket salad.' But instead of getting marks for initiative, technique, presentation and taste, she just pointed out that I was flambéing with brandy and pupils weren't allowed to bring alcohol to school. Ah yes, that.

The benefits of my French work experience placements may have been totally lost on that occasion, but when it really mattered they were spotted immediately. My first week at catering college, when I was 16, was a defining moment in my life. I wasn't starting further education with ambitions to be a star pupil. I'd been at Scarborough Technical College for a couple of days when the head lecturer, a guy called Ken Allanson, who's still a great friend of mine, came to give the new intake of students the once-over. Ken taught the third years, who were like the SAS of the catering college. At the start of the first year there were 120 numpties, most of whom thought a bit of cooking would be an easy option. By year two that number was nearly halved to those who were quite serious about it, but by year three all that were left were the dozen or so hardcore students who desperately wanted to do it as a career. Those are the students Ken taught, so when he came into the room everyone was shitting themselves.

We were all there, immaculate in our starched-to-buggery jackets which were as stiff as boards (so stiff you couldn't move your arms in them), with our overstarched tea towels that wouldn't soak up anything, all dressed to impressed, and Ken, who had been walking around watching us during the lesson, came up, put his arm round me and said, 'You're not a bad cook, are you?'

I was 16. No one had ever before had a good word to say about me in a classroom. I was absolutely bricking it.

'No, chef,' I said.

He nodded, smiled and added, 'I'll have to keep my eye on you.'

And that was it, probably the defining moment of my life and career. That one compliment made me suddenly believe I might actually be able to do this, not in an arrogant way but in an I-can-make-something-of-myself-after-all kind of a way. I knew from that moment on that it was worth getting my head down. True to his word, Ken kept his eye on me throughout college, always steered me in the right direction, and saw me being offered jobs by practically every one of the top chefs who came to judge my year's final exam.

I pretty much owe my entire career to Ken Allanson. He managed to keep me humble and hungry enough to learn while building my confidence and self-belief. But most of all I owe him for spotting the excitement and passion those French wine trips had instilled in me, and for undoing all the damage my uncharitable and unforgiving former cookery teacher had done over the years. In the time it took Ken to come over and say those few kind words, the inside of my head completely changed. I went from bottom of the class to number one; from the one who'd never get anywhere to the one to watch. I'd known since the age of seven that I wanted to be a chef, but if I had to narrow it down and pick a moment when I knew for sure it was what I was going to do with my life, well, that was the one.

10 'EXTRA-CURRICULAR': THE WHITE VAUXHALL NOVA

The first car I had was a white Vauxhall Nova, 950cc, the one with the boot on the back that no one wanted. My dad paid £250 for it. It was a cut'n'shunt job: not two, but three smashed-up cars welded together. Although I'm not sure why they bothered, or why, if they were going to all that trouble, they didn't pick the more attractive hatchback option for the back end. Or, for that matter, why they didn't pick a better interior: it had the same horrible brown chocolate-crumb-magnet cloth as my dad's old Ford Capri Laser 1.6. Still, while it was definitely a complete crock of shit, and probably bloody dangerous, aside from a couple of weeks during which it was in for repairs, it was a loyal and reliable thing. It got me through catering college. I had it all the time I was working in London, too, which was nearly two years. It even survived a car park crash on my first day at Chewton Glen, one of the most prestigious hotels in the UK. Of all the cars I've owned, I had that white Nova the longest. It saw me go from young, enthusiastic and unqualified practically all the way through to becoming a head chef. And that's a lot of action. Though not the most glamorous or exciting of cars, it was an important one.

For the first month after passing my test I drove the Nova the 40 miles from home to college every day. Eventually my mum said that I really needed to get digs because travelling backwards and forwards was ridiculous, so I found a place with my old school mate David Coates, who was also at Scarborough doing catering, and another bloke called Malcolm. The flat was above, of all places, Henry Marshall's amusement arcade on Scarborough seafront, the same Henry Marshall's where I'd seen my first Aston Martin V8 Vantage nine years earlier. But I would still drive back home in the Nova every weekend to work in the kitchens at Castle Howard or to cater for functions for my dad's friends.

I was bombing it back from college one Friday night, about midnight, when I almost ran into our local bobby. It was dark, I was driving too fast, and I came tearing round this corner and he was just sat there in his car, glaring headlights, eyes out on stalks, looking like he had myxomatosis, with a sandwich in his gob. I came round this corner sideways, just missed him, straightened up and drove as fast as I could up through the village. I knew he'd know exactly who it was – it was a very small village – but being 17 and not thinking straight I drove home, straight through the gates of the farm, turned the lights off and then drove about a mile and a half up this track, thinking that he'd never follow me up there. I then ran back to the farm and hid in the pig sheds.

By then our friendly neighbourhood policeman was already in the house, talking to Dad, who was going, 'I'll find him, he's here somewhere.' I got a right bollocking that night when I did eventually summon up the courage to go in the house. My dad was sitting there, cup of coffee in his hand, and he just looked at me and said, 'Now, tell me what happened.' I knew I was in big trouble.

I spent practically my entire student grant on that car. I bought a Panasonic tape deck and speakers so I could play my Rick Astley and Jason Donovan tapes nice and loud, and I got some new push-on plastic wheel covers. It wasn't really tricking it out, just trying to make it look better. The rest of the grant went on alcohol. In Scarborough, as in most student towns, Thursday night was student night and we all used to get completely shitfaced on Taboo and lemonade.

With the stereo on and Bryan Adams's 'Summer of '69' blaring out, me and my mates went cruising. We used to drive up and down Scarborough seafront, and then around Malton Market, where all the young farmers were in their tricked-out Vauxhall Novas, bombing it around the market square, accelerating and braking over the speed humps. They still do it today. If you go to Malton Market on a Friday or Saturday night you'll find it full of these lads in their pimped-up Corsas with neon lights and chrome rims, bouncing about the place while the girls point and get very excited. Because my Nova was never properly tricked out, most of the time we stuck to cruising, or I used to go up the

North Yorkshire Moors at night and just blat it, fifth gear, flat out, drifting sideways, being careful to avoid the sheep which tended to stand in the middle of the road. When I wasn't driving the Nova I was circling the Golf GTis, XR2s and Audi Quattros in *AutoTrader* and *Exchange & Mart* wondering how much I'd get in part exchange for it. 'Nothing' was the answer, but I didn't know that back then.

The only other car I drove at that time was my dad's work car, a Ford Cortina estate. I borrowed it when the Nova was in for repairs after I'd skidded on some ice and dinged the front underside spoiler. The Cortina was pretty cool, probably the coolest car my dad ever owned. It wasn't the best car in the world but it was newer than mine and it had a better stereo. There were two roundabouts, one at either end of the seafront, and we used to just drive backwards and forwards, up to one roundabout, round and back to the other, all afternoon. Driving along with all my mates in it, cruising up and down, that car felt like a pimp wagon. Of course, being an estate, it also had other uses.

I never really had a girlfriend until I was 17. That I got one even then was pretty much down to an image makeover by my mum. One day, quite out of the blue, she decided that we all needed to get some sun, so we went to Corfu for a week's holiday. When we came back, looking all tanned and healthy, she suddenly got it into her head that I should dress like Jason Donovan. She'd seen him on TV wearing a black hat, black shirt with white spots, jeans and beige boots, and she thought the look would suit me. With that I was off down the hairdresser's to have some highlights and my hair cut just like Jason's. I got the black hat, which I perched on the back of my head, the black shirt with the white spots, the jeans and the boots; I even had the little quiff of hair at the front. With my tan, I thought I looked pretty bloody cool.

And like magic, I started going out with Annie, the most beautiful girl in school.

Annie was in the class next to mine at catering college. Obviously, she liked the Jason Donovan look because she'd never paid me much attention before. She lived in a B&B, which was a better bet for any 'extra-curricular activity' than my digs: our landlady used to listen outside the door at night to make sure the three of us lads hadn't brought any girls back and weren't getting up to any funny stuff. For extra privacy, though, the old Cortina estate came in very handy.

Our relationship progressed and one thing led to another, as it usually does, and one memorable night Annie and I went off in the Cortina for a drive up to the appropriately named Oliver's Mount. By day this was nothing but a hill with a motorbike dirt track and a TV mast on it; by night it was a dark and deserted love nest! So with a twinkle in my eye and my Jason Donovan hat perched on my head I drove up Oliver's Mount with Annie beside me. A whole fifteen minutes later, the deed done, we drove back down again. Fast forward, and years later Jason Donovan came on *Saturday Kitchen*. After the show I told him this story about how I owed losing my virginity to him and his taste in shirts. He looked at me a bit weird, so I told him the tale. Then he looked at me a little uncomfortably, smiled and said, 'I'm very pleased for you.'

Catering college wasn't all girls and cars and Taboo and lemonade though, it was a lot of hard work too. Never more so than when it came to the six-week work experience placements in France. They were hard. The first year wasn't so bad. Just 14 of us were picked to go over to Pornic near Brittany for the summer. Only the most promising students were invited because we'd be working in the kitchens of two-star Michelin restaurants, so there wasn't room for anyone who was just making up the numbers. It was nothing like the fantastic, inspiring experiences I'd had in the chateaux of the South of France when my dad was doing the wine run to Saint Emilion. That first year I spent almost the entire time peeling potatoes in a fish restaurant. Still, it was a privilege to be there.

The second year, though, that was something else. We had better placements, but they were much harder. Each of us was on our own, one student per restaurant, and we didn't really have any time to meet up. I was working 18-hour days in a kitchen full of French chefs who hated the English. Absolutely hated us. As far as they were concerned, in the food world the English were the lowest of the low and didn't even deserve to set foot in their restaurant. We were all roast beef and Berni Inns and nothing else, which certainly had been true in the past, though in recent years British cooking had come up a lot. I think that also put their noses out of joint a bit. So for 18 hours a day I was stood on a spot no bigger than four floor tiles, facing the wall, and I had to peel and turn carrots all day long. I wasn't allowed to turn around, speak or go to the toilet without asking. There was another English student from another college there, and while we were facing the wall, doing our work, the rest of the kitchen would throw things at us, knock into us with sharp-cornered trays, bash us with boiling-hot pans, shout and hurl abuse. It was horrendous.

Thanks to my father's refusal to pull me out of school when I was being bullied, I've always had a don't-let-them-grind-you-down mentality; the other thing I got from my father was a very definite breaking point. You can only push me so far before I'll come back at you, and four weeks into the placement I reached my limit. I was bruised and burnt and covered in cuts, so when I had a boiling-hot pan thrown at me I calmly put down my knife, slotted it back into my knife roll and took off my apron. The sous chef went nuts. 'Wat doo yoo sink yoo ahh doingg?' he screamed at me. 'Where doo yoo sink yoo ahh goingg?' I replied by walking up to him and throwing a right hook that launched him right over the hot plate. I then turned round, calmly walked out of the back door of the restaurant and ran like my life depended on it across the fields, terrified that I was about to get lynched by a brigade of angry meat-cleaver-wielding French chefs. I ran straight to our lecturer to say that I'd had enough, but by then he'd already had a call saying I wasn't welcome back. That was a hard, hard experience for a 17-year-old, but it was probably one of the best things that ever happened to me because it was invaluable training for what I was about to experience working in London.

Thankfully, flooring the sous chef while on work experience didn't have a negative impact on the rest of my time at catering college, or my qualifications. I was student of the year three years running, thanks in part to my love of fat carvings and sugar work (since the age of ten I'd carved sculptures out of butter and worked hot sugar into glass decorations). When Brian Turner and Keith Floyd came to cook at our college dinners I was picked to work in the kitchens alongside them – my first real experience of 'celebrity chefs'. I say cook. I think I only saw Keith in the kitchen twice, the rest of the evening he was in the bar. When he stood up to make a speech he told everyone to 'fuck off' then got in his white Rolls-Royce and drove off. Legend.

After several years of guidance from Ken Allanson and the other lecturers, I was offered jobs at some of the best restaurants in London. Back then, Scarborough and Westminster were the two best catering colleges in the country. Scarborough had an amazing reputation because of its shit-hot lecturers, so we were able to get the best chefs, including Alastair Little, Stephen Bull, Brian Turner, David Dorricott and Antony Worrall Thompson, to come and judge our end-of-year exam. The exam wasn't actually part of the catering qualification itself, it didn't have a bearing on whether or not you passed the course and got your diploma, but it did have a bearing on whether or not you got a good job. Each of us was given a trolley of ingredients and six hours to cook a range of classic dishes. It was all pretty standard stuff, but how you made them and how you chose to present them was down to you. You were competing against yourself as well as your classmates, and you were out to impress. Considering there were only maybe a dozen of us left out of the crowd that had started the course three years earlier, it was a great opportunity to stand out and get spotted.

I was pretty happy with what I'd done, and afterwards Ken came up to me and said, 'You know they're probably all going to offer you a job.' Sure enough, each of them came round, asked what my plans were, gave me their cards and told me to call them.

I had no idea what to do. I'd been hopeful of being offered something, but it had never occurred to me that I'd be offered more than one post. I had a chat with Ken, who said that the top student the year before had gone to Antony Worrall Thompson's restaurant, One Ninety Queen's Gate in Kensington, and that he'd done well there, had a good experience, enjoyed it and was about to leave. So I said, 'I'll go there then.'

A few weeks later, on the Friday I finished college for good, I went home and packed up my stuff. First thing Monday morning I made my way to London to start at One Ninety Queen's Gate.

11 *THE GOOD, THE BAD AND THE UGLY*

When I'd first come to London, for six-week's work experience in a hotel restaurant on Park Lane, I was only 14. It was there that I learned the Good, the Bad and the Ugly of the capital city. The Good was that London had the most amazing cars in the showrooms of Park Lane and Berkeley Square, which I used to go and walk past on my breaks. The Bad was how some of the chefs treated the food. The Ugly was how some of the chefs treated the staff. I saw some great cars in those garages and I saw some terrible shit happen in those kitchens, so I had a vague idea of what to expect when I returned to London after college to work for Antony Worrall Thompson. I'd felt the fury and the boiling pots of French chefs, so it wasn't like I didn't know how to survive a brutal 18-hour day. Still, nothing could have prepared me for what lay ahead.

My parents and my sister took me to Malton station to see me off. My mum was in tears, my sister didn't give a toss, and my dad was, well, my dad. As I was standing on the platform about to get on the train for London he put out his arm. I thought for a second he was about to hug me, which as far as I could remember was something he'd never done before. Instead he shook me by the hand, and as he did so he thrust a piece of paper into my palm. I knew instantly it was a cheque and I slipped it straight into my pocket without even looking. I said, 'Thanks, Dad,' and he said, 'That'll see you all right. Now, good luck, son. I won't see you for a while, but take care of yourself.'

I got on the train and stood there, leaning out the window, waving as the train pulled out. When I sat down I felt inside my pocket for the cheque, feeling bloody relieved because I only had about £200 in my bank account and I knew that wasn't going to last in London. I pulled it out of my pocket, and my heart sank when I realised it wasn't a cheque at all, but a crisp £50 note. Fifty quid. Was that it? What good was that going to be? I was looking at the note in disbelief at just how tight my dad had been when I noticed, written on one side, a message from my father: 'Now fuck off, and I don't want to see you again for at least two years.' Bloody hell. Looking back, of all his attempts at character building, forcing me to stand on my feet like that was probably one of the best things he ever did for me. But it didn't feel like it at the time.

When I got to King's Cross I got in a black cab and asked the driver to take me to One Ninety Queen's Gate. Then I watched as the numbers on the meter went up and up and up. It was a fiver before we'd got to the end of the street. I've had an issue with black cabs ever since. I remember looking out the window as we sat in the traffic, thinking how incredibly big and busy and noisy London was, and how wherever you looked people seemed to be in a rush. Although I was not a stranger to London, it seemed bigger, busier and noisier than I remembered it. By the time we got to the restaurant the meter was reading £22. I handed over my only cash, the note my dad had given me, being careful to make sure his message was facing down. I felt sick when the cabbie handed back my £28 change.

I walked into the restaurant, which is in the Gore Hotel, just around the corner from the Royal Albert Hall, and introduced myself to one of the waiters who told me to wait in the bar while he went off to get Antony. The bar was 'olde-worlde', all beautiful dark oak. I was looking around and suddenly I thought, 'I recognise that person over there.' I tried to place him, and then it hit me. It was the guy from Right Said Fred, and this was in the days when they were huge. When I went to sit in the other corner of the bar I saw the singer of the Commitments, who I found out later were living in the hotel. I just thought that was so cool.

It must have been a good hour before Antony finally came through wearing one of his trademark garishly hand-painted waistcoats. He shook my hand and asked who I was. I gave him my name and explained that I was starting today, that I was from Scarborough Tech and that he'd offered me a job. I showed him the letter confirming the post and he said, 'Oh yes, yes, yes, I remember. Right, where are you staying?' I told him I didn't have anywhere and he said not to worry, Troy would sort me out.

Troy was summoned, and two minutes later a really loud American in clogs came clomping up the stairs. He looked absolutely dreadful. He had big black rings around his eyes like he hadn't slept in weeks, his hair was all over the place, and he had a dirty blue apron on. I just couldn't believe the state of him. He introduced himself, said he'd sort me somewhere to stay, then asked if I wanted to work now. Me being keen, I said, 'Yeah, yeah, cool,' and within half an hour I was in the changing room, which like all changing rooms in all restaurants smelt of dirty old aprons. I was soon dressed in my lovely clean chef's whites and under my arm I had my roll of chef's knives, all of which had been engraved with my name so no one could nick them when I was at college. I was looking all smart and tidy and straight out of college.

I walked into the kitchen and what looked like the most frantic service I'd ever seen in a restaurant was going on. Then I looked at my watch. It was only three o'clock in the afternoon, service hadn't even started yet. That should have warned me.

It was manic in that kitchen, and a lot to take in. There was a huge bloke with massive muscles bulging out of his T-shirt standing at the sink, which was loaded high with great dirty piles of crap. He was a Brazilian power lifting champion and pot washer. There was a little foreign guy at the other sink who was the other pot washer; he was surrounded by similarly high piles of crap. Troy was cooking at a stove with a load of pans in front of him. The larder section, which was really just a fridge with a worktop on it, was in chaos. Honestly, I'd walked into absolute mayhem.

Troy told me that I'd be starting on the pastry section and he led me round to the back room, which had an oven and a little bench in it. He introduced me to Stephen, the pastry chef, whom I'd be working under. And it was straight in; no showing you around and telling you where everything was or anything. Stephen just said, 'Can you make me some lemon tarts? There's the pastry. Roll them out, bake them blind and then we'll fill them in a bit.' I'd been there literally ten minutes and I was already making lemon tarts. Next to me on the other side there were these two Portuguese butchers hammering meat and sending bone fragments flying everywhere. I was picking bits of bone out of my pastry left, right and centre. I didn't want to say anything, so I picked up a tray that was on the side and wedged it in next to me like a shield to protect my pastry. That worked, an awkward situation was averted, and I soon began to feel surprisingly comfortable. I knew what I was doing. Everything felt under control.

I baked the pastry cases, which came out great, and then I started on the filling. Now, at college, when we made lemon tarts we used ten eggs. But the recipe Stephen gave me called for 180 eggs, along with 4 kilos of sugar, 100 lemons (zest and juice) and 12 litres of double cream. I thought, 'How the hell am I going to make this?'

'Do you want me to break this down?' I asked Stephen.

'No,' he replied, 'that's how much I want you to do.'

'Holy crap,' I thought. 'I've got to break 180 eggs.' That's when I learned to break eggs with one in each hand. It took me about three hours of zesting and squeezing lemons, cracking eggs and mixing to make that first batch of lemon tarts. Four weeks later I could do it in 15 minutes.

The second day I was working on the pastry section again, still just getting my head around where everything was and how the place worked, because there were two restaurants, the main one downstairs and an even busier bistro upstairs, and the pastry section served both. About eleven am, Stephen said he was going to the loo. About an hour later Troy came in and said, 'Where's Stephen?' I said he'd gone to the toilet a while back. Troy asked if his knives were still there. I looked under the counter: they'd gone. We went to the changing room and checked his locker. It was empty. He'd gone. Walked out. I never saw him again. On my second day at One Ninety Queen's Gate I was promoted to head pastry chef.

As I later found out, this used to happen a couple of times a week. On average, half the kitchen brigade would walk because it was such hard work and they'd just had enough. You learned that if someone said they were going to the loo you had to check if their knives were still there. If they weren't, you knew you were going to be a man down. We used to get through staff like we were shelling peas. After about six months of working there I discovered that other restaurants called us the Mad Army, whilst Langham's was known as the Lunatic Asylum. The crazy pace that everyone worked at meant that there was a high turnover of staff in every restaurant. One day this guy on the stove just collapsed right in front of me, in the middle of service. Not used to seeing people just keel over, I called for help and was told basically just to get on with it and leave him to it. And he stayed down on the floor until he came to his senses enough to get up and start cooking again. That's just what used to happen. You'd work hard and then you'd collapse because you hadn't eaten or hadn't had a break in maybe eight hours.

There were chefs all over London who dealt with it by snorting coke or shooting up. I never did drugs, but I knew plenty who did. That was the first time I came into contact with them. People would do a line of coke before service, just to get through it. I remember one guy used to come in, eyes wide, completely wired, and I used to think, 'How come he's so awake?' We'd all worked 18 hours the day before and there he was, first thing, buzzing. He'd go on to do the work of three people. Innocent country boy that I was, it took me ages to work out where he got all his energy from.

There were no split shifts, we just used to work straight through. If you were lucky you worked seven am to five pm; if things were busy it might be seven am to one am the next morning. We did that six days a week. That was our life. I was there just over a year, on £5,000 – no minimum wage in those days. I think my mum worked out once that I was on about 88p an hour, or something ridiculous like that. To give you an idea what that translated as, when Michael Jackson released his *Dangerous* album it took me a whole month to save up to buy it. I couldn't afford a travelcard in London, never mind a car, so the Nova stayed at home and I walked everywhere. From One Ninety Queen's Gate to Piccadilly to Covent Garden, wherever, I just used to get a can of Coke and walk.

Of course, I continued my practice of peering through the windows of all the big car showrooms. I knew every garage off by heart because I walked past them all. The restaurant wasn't open Saturday mornings so I used to walk from the flat I shared with a load of chefs in Queensway, along the Bayswater Road and down Park Lane to look through the showroom windows at the Aston Martins and Jaguars and the McLaren F1 which was on display where Harrods Estates is now. Once I was done there, I'd head down Piccadilly towards the Ritz and up into Berkeley Square to check out the Porsche dealership and to press my nose against the window of Jack Barclay's and stare at the Bentleys. I literally knew my way around London by restaurants and car dealerships. The dealer opposite Bibendum on Brompton Cross was always full of Ferraris. Round the corner from One Ninety Queen's Gate were Coys and Fiskens, who both sold vintage cars, as did Hall & Bradfield a few blocks over in South Kensington. It was how I would entertain myself on those rare days or mornings off, or late at night when there was no one else around. Standing outside Coys breathing on the glass and looking at the Ferrari F40s all lit up inside was cheaper than buying a TV.

We were working so long and so hard that the first time my mum came to visit, she didn't recognise me. She came to the restaurant and literally walked straight past me. I was down to 8½ stone, which considering I'm 6 ft 3 in wasn't good. I looked like shit. In fact, I looked like Troy had looked when I first saw him four months earlier. I'd started to black out from lack of food and sleep. I was a state. Mum must have been frantic.

We weren't the only ones working all hours. There was a KFC by the Kensington Place restaurant that stayed open until three am purely to serve chefs. If you went in there on a Friday or Saturday night it was full of chefs and prostitutes. But unlike the prostitutes we couldn't afford a bargain bucket. As we walked home, the working girls used to proposition us. 'All right, love? Fancy a bit of fun?' But they were out of luck touting for business with chefs. Even if we did fancy a bit of fun, there was no way any of us could afford it, let alone have the energy for it.

You had no relationships, you had no friends; the only people you knew were the people you worked with in the kitchen, and they kept leaving. You basically had no life. The longer you work in an environment like that the more you become a part of it, and I was becoming just as rude and aggressive as everyone else. Antony had just started doing TV, appearing on a programme called *Hot Chefs*, so the restaurant was packed and the pressure was on.

Celebrity chefs weren't commonplace back then, it was just Delia and Floyd cooking kievs and muffins, so little did I know what would happen some years later. But One Ninety Queen's Gate was like The Ivy is now, 'the' celeb haunt. Stars like Shirley Bassey and Princess Diana dined and stood at the bar along with the hundreds of others waiting for a table, many queuing outside. The bar was the best bit – as we wandered round outside the bistro, wearing our dirty chef's whites and with our arms full of trays of bread and butter pudding, we'd have one eye on the mini-skirts and the champagne flutes, whilst the other was people-spotting in the bar. Every night, famous pop singers would grab the karaoke mike from behind the bar and blast out their latest top-ten tune. Bros, Paul Young, The Commitments – they were all in there, drinking five-quid-a-glass bubbly. I couldn't even afford the peanuts. While *Deeply Dippy* sounded out on the mike, both the restaurant and the bar were heaving. From eleven am to two pm the place just kept filling up as fast as the wine glasses. I've always loved the buzz of places like this, all sparkles and spandex, but though it was great to watch, I knew if ever I had the chance to join in, it just wasn't the place for me. I felt far more comfortable in the kitchen than I ever did outside with the guests, and I feel the same even now. The kitchen is my territory. I don't know whether it's something to do with the heat or the pressure (it's not the money, that's for sure!) but to anyone else looking in from the outside, they'd probably think me just plain mad.

It was a mental place to work, One Ninety Queen's Gate, but it wasn't unique or anywhere near the hardest kitchen I would work in before finally leaving London for good. I later spent a few weeks in a West End restaurant, which has since closed. That was truly insane. Totally deranged. I ruined a crème Anglaise sauce once, a simple thing to do:

you let it get just 4 degrees too hot and it'll separate. There is a way to bring it back – you add double cream to it – but because I was using it for ice cream I knew that when I churned it, it would go grainy, so I binned the lot. The owner saw me do it and went nuts. It was his restaurant, his money, I'd just wasted two dozen of his eggs, and now he was going to kill me. So he set about me, and he didn't stop until I had a broken collar bone and two broken ribs. When I turned up for work the next day I'm not sure who was more surprised, him or me, but there was no way I was going to let him break me.

After a year and a half in London, I felt I'd done my time and had got about as much as I was going to get out of being there; I also felt I'd probably do myself or someone else some harm if I stayed much longer. When you think that on average most people lasted three weeks, I'd done pretty well. I was young, I wanted to learn more, and I wanted to move on. At the time, Marco Pierre White was the hot thing. He'd just brought out a book called *White Heat* and everyone wanted to go and work at his restaurant, Harvey's, in Wandsworth Common. Antony knew him, so I asked if he'd put in a good word for me. He gave Marco a ring and came back saying that I should go to Marco's restaurant on Saturday morning.

Walking into Harvey's was like walking into a totally different world. There was mayhem, but it wasn't crazy like One Ninety Queen's Gate. This was a 40-cover fine dining restaurant, the most talked-about establishment in the UK at that time, three-star Michelin. I was shitting myself. I remember sitting there in the glass-covered reception area with my heart going mental. Sure enough, Marco, who was the *enfant terrible* of cooking, came out in a blue and white apron, hair everywhere, fag in his gob. He sat down, and immediately I was aware that there was something about him, an incredible presence. He was very abrupt, wanted to know where I'd been working, what I was doing. I told him that I was at One Ninety Queen's Gate and was looking for the next step, and he said, 'Well, you can work here, but I'm not paying you.'

Now, I really wanted to work there, so I said, 'Fine,' thinking I'd work out how I was going to manage later. Of course I started to get into debt quite badly, but it was an amazing experience and worth every penny. It was totally different to One Ninety Queen's Gate. Harvey's was my first experience of proper Michelin star cooking, and this was three stars. The pressure was totally on Marco. It was quiet in the kitchen but if anything went wrong he'd kick off majorly, shouting, screaming, throwing pans everywhere, and when that happened you paid attention. This wasn't some prima donna having a tantrum, this was a perfection-ist demanding the best. I learned so much. In my previous job I'd learned to cook quickly; this was about cooking brilliantly. At One Ninety Queen's Gate we could do 200 covers in the bistro and 100 in the restaurant; at Harvey's you did 40. We were doing fewer covers but there was more work because the food was far more difficult to prepare, much more complex, and everything was made fresh twice a day. At One Ninety Queen's Gate I was used to making

18 lemon tarts and that would suffice for lunch and dinner; at Harvey's it had to be a fresh tart baked just before service, and when it was gone it was gone. You had to cook another for the next service. Everything had to be perfect. The carrots perfectly diced, the salmon, the sea bass, every portion perfect.

It was a great experience, but after six weeks I just couldn't afford to stay there any longer. I asked Marco if he had any full-time jobs on the payroll. He didn't, which was understandable, because everyone wanted to work there. Those posts were so coveted no one was ever going to leave. But he told me he had a mate, Phil Howard, who ran The Square on Berkeley Square (which I knew because of my trips to Jack Barclay's Bentley showroom) who might be able to give me something. He'd put a word in.

I went to The Square, which was two-star Michelin, and Phil was great. He took me on, but again, he couldn't pay me. I stuck at it for about three weeks, but by then I'd racked up about eight grand's worth of debt, just in living expenses. I wasn't spending anything else; I didn't have the time. My rent was £700 a month and my overdraft could only take so much.

One of the chefs at The Square said a mate of his was the head chef of Stephen Bull's new restaurant in Smithfield Market, and again he put in a word for me. I went to meet Stephen, who offered me a job in what had to be the smallest kitchen in the world. It was 6 feet by 10 feet, if that, and crazily busy serving classic Italian bistro food, all pastas and risottos. Great food it was, much quicker than at Harvey's or The Square. That was a really good job, and it was paid, but I think by that point I'd had enough of London. My debts quickly rose to the tune of something like eleven grand and I just woke up one morning and thought, 'I'm fucked. I've got no money and I'm fucked.' There really is nothing more depressing than working your nuts off and never having any money.

My mum was pulling her hair out, getting more and more depressed watching me going down and down. I was physically screwed, around 9 stone in weight, and I'd collapse once a month from exhaustion. Mentally, too, I was low. I used to just sit at home and cry when I got in from work because I had no friends, no money, no life. I was 20 and thinking, 'What the hell am I doing?' I knew I had to go through the mill to achieve my ambitions, but I just couldn't do it any more.

I didn't have the balls to go to my folks and ask to borrow some money, as they'd been sending me M&S food vouchers to live on, so after nearly two years of 18-hour days and six-day weeks I finally packed my bag, asked my dad to meet me at the station, and went home.

12 A NEW START IN THE NEW FOREST

London had been brutal, exhausting and demoralising. I had worked in some of the best kitchens with some of the best chefs. I'd learned to cook exceptional food to an exceptional standard, and exceptionally quickly. I'd learned important lessons that would stand me in good stead for when I became a head chef myself, but the process had left me so knackered that even standing up itself was almost out of the question. When I got back to Yorkshire I slept for the first 48 hours straight. That's how tired I was. I stayed at home for a couple of weeks, jobless and with no idea of what to do next.

When I finally had enough energy to think about work again, I got in touch with my old lecturer Ken Allanson, who suggested that as I'd worked in some of the best bistros and restaurants in the world it made sense to go and work in one of the best hotels; that way I'd be able to work absolutely anywhere I wanted to in the future. I told him there was no way I could go back to London – I'd been there, done that and had eleven grand's worth of debt to prove it – so we got out a copy of *The Good Food Guide* and circled the best hotels outside London.

There were three five-star hotels – Gleneagles, Chewton Glen and Gidleigh Park – and I wrote letters to all three, enclosing copies of my CV. Five days later I got two letters back. Gleneagles: sorry, no vacancies. Gidleigh Park: same thing, only it was a personal letter from Shaun Hill, a top, top chef, two Michelin stars, whom everyone looked up to (Shaun and I know each other now and he always jokes that there's a job there for me if I still want it). Chewton Glen was my last hope or it was back to the drawing board. Next day, I got a letter from them asking if I'd be interested in the position of junior pastry chef.

Interested?!? Chewton Glen is a luxury hotel and spa on the edge of the New Forest in Hampshire. It has been voted one of the top ten hotels in the world; it has five red AA stars and five RAC stars with gold ribbon; it held a Michelin star for a staggering 27 consecutive years. Rooms cost between £400 and £1,500 a night. Yes, I was interested.

I drove down in the Nova from Yorkshire to the New Forest for the interview, and met the chef, an amazing and eccentric guy called Pierre Chevillard who walked me into this beautiful, massive kitchen. Though I was still only 20 years old, I'd seen a lot of kitchens in my time, but nothing like this one at Chewton Glen. It had gleaming white floor tiles and a big central cooking isle surrounded by chefs who looked nothing like me. I looked like shit, like something from *Night of the Living Dead*; these guys were all bright-eyed, clean and smart. On the downside, they were all French, and given my last experience of cooking with a French brigade, this was a bit daunting. There were 52 chefs in the kitchen, and only five were English. I was going for junior pastry chef, which effectively made me sixth in command, but I was also the second youngest in there, so although it was clearly far more civilised than a lot of the places I'd worked in I still had a lot to prove.

After seeing just the kitchen I was sold on the place. When I got the guided tour of the rest of the hotel, the restaurant, the health club, the spa, the helipad, the grounds and the golf course I was convinced it really was for me, not so much because of the place itself but because someone had actually taken the time to show me round. Truly, I'd never experienced anything like that in my professional life before.

I worked the lunch service to see if it suited me. There were nine of us in the pastry section and we did just 32 covers for lunch. I liked it all right! At the end of the service Pierre said that he thought I'd fit in, that I'd like it there, and he wanted to offer me the job. He said that they worked split shifts, usually nine to three and then back again from six to anything as late as ten pm. Only ten pm? I couldn't sign up fast enough.

A week later I dumped all my stuff in the digs they'd sorted out for me – £30 a week, sharing with one other bloke and six girls; I couldn't believe my luck! I jumped in the Nova and drove to work, up the drive, past the tennis courts on the right, past all these gorgeous Victorian street lamps, over a little bridge, past the stunning manicured lawns that surround the health club, and into the car park. Unfortunately, when I was being given the guided tour no one mentioned there was more than one car park. There was the health club car park on the left, the staff car park (which I knew nothing about) on the right and the main car park right in front of me, which was full of Mercedes and Bentleys.

I spotted this amazing-looking girl walking across the car park, with a great tan and quite considerable assets squeezed into a white beauty therapist's uniform. She was stunning. I was having a good look, mesmerised, when, BANG! I drove straight into one of the gorgeous Victorian lamp posts. Worse than that, its antique top fell off, rebounded off the top of the Nova and landed in the middle of the car park. The car had bounced over the kerb, which had ripped off the entire underside, and come to rest right outside the front door of the prestigious Chewton Glen Hotel.

There was oil pissing out all over the gravel and I was sitting there, having just arrived for my first day at work, wondering what the hell had just happened. Next thing I knew, the owner of Chewton Glen, a fantastic man by the name of Martin Skan who's still a good friend, came rushing out, not to abuse me for wrecking his lamp post and covering his car park in oil but to see if I was all right. I said I was, and I introduced myself, explaining that it was my first day working in the kitchen. He smiled, put out his hand and said, 'Welcome to Chewton Glen, James.'

After slogging my guts out in London for nearly two years, working there was like staying in a holiday camp. It wasn't just the guests who were living in the lap of luxury, compared to what I was used to the staff were treated like royalty too, or at the very least like regular human beings. Split shifts, days off, holidays ... I don't think anyone there knew the meaning of an 18-hour day. From the moment I 'parked' my white Vauxhall Nova that first day I knew I'd made the right decision. Compared to the Michelin-starred London kitchens where I was used to getting my arse kicked, being at Chewton Glen was literally like coming out for a weekend in the country. Everything about the place worked at a slower, more human pace, including the kitchen.

That didn't always sit well with me. For one, I didn't get on with one of the pastry chefs because I thought he was so bloody lazy. I was used to working my nuts off and I expected everybody else in the pastry section to be doing the same, and they did, except this guy. Instead of doing something useful he would spend the whole day sketching designs for new chocolate cakes. He used to roll in late and leave early. I couldn't respect him, so the only raised voices you'd ever hear in this normally placid kitchen were him and me arguing over why he wasn't doing his job properly.

We finally fell out over frozen jelly. Rather than make everything fresh before each service, as all Michelin-starred restaurants would, he wanted to stock up on things during quiet times and freeze them so we'd never be really pushed or stretched. Just a few months prior to my arrival the

Chewton Glen restaurant had lost the Michelin star it had held for over a quarter of a century. I was part of a new influx of staff brought in with the aim of winning it back. I think they lost their Michelin star because of this sort of attitude. It got so bad between me and him that we came to physical blows, and while the head chef and the sous chef didn't want to let me go, they couldn't sack him either, so they moved me to the larder, fish and sauce section.

The other guy's attitude was even more infuriating because the head chef was such a perfectionist. He was an absolute genius, but as with all geniuses he was also completely bonkers, and as the restaurant got busier he found it harder to achieve the level of brilliance he was searching for and would end up, literally, smacking his head again and again against the check board where all the orders were put. You didn't want to be there when he started head-butting the board. There'd be checks and orders flying all over the place. You'd have no idea what was waiting, what was done, what order any of it was meant to be in. You'd be there desperately trying to work out what was what, trying to piece it all back together and stop the whole thing descending into the shit, and chef would still be banging his head against the board because he just couldn't balance his need for perfection with the need to get through the covers. He was a truly brilliant chef though, a man to whom, alongside Ken Allanson, I owe my career.

Infuriating as the laziness of some was, the more relaxed pace of the kitchen did have its compensations. All of a sudden I had a life again. I could drive out in my little Nova to Bradshaw's in Bournemouth and Meridian in the New Forest to look at the Ferraris, and over to Westover Cars in Salisbury to look at the Lotuses. In fact, I had so much time to go driving that within about four months of starting at Chewton Glen I'd sold the Nova and taken a step up in the world to a 1.1 Ford Fiesta (which I soon changed for a 1.9 Diesel).

And then there were the girls. Literally, there were women everywhere at Chewton Glen. Waitresses, beauty therapists, hair stylists, receptionists – I'd never seen so many girls. Much to my surprise, I got my fair share of female attention, some of it welcome, some of it not so. All of it, though, was very, very insistent.

First there was Genevieve, one of the waitresses. Genevieve was incredibly posh with an amazing figure, but I just didn't fancy her. One night after service she informed me that I was going to take her out to eat. I wasn't really interested, but I didn't like to say so, so I said I'd be happy to take her out, just as soon as I'd finished rolling my truffles. Now, as anyone who's ever worked the pastry section of a restaurant will tell you, rolling truffles is one of the longest, most laborious jobs there is. This batch took me four and a half hours, during which time she lost interest and took herself out to eat.

Then there was Tana, one of the hairdressers. She was blonde and stunning all the way to the top, and this time I was definitely interested. Again she told me we were going on a date, more specifically that I was going to cook for her.

She said she'd meet me at my place at ten. I worked like crazy that night, I pushed and pushed to get out by nine so I'd have time to cook her something really special. Before leaving I grabbed a couple of slices of the terrine from the larder and something from our section for dessert, so all I had to do was nip into the supermarket on my way back to get something for our main course. Of course, just my luck, the supermarket was closed when I got there. It was a Sunday night. The only other place I could think of that would be open was the petrol station. I got there, looked around, and all they had was an onion, a couple of manky bits of mushroom, some streaky bacon and cheap (£2.99) bottles of plonk. It was like an early audition for *Ready Steady Cook*.

I was trying to think what I could do with this miserable selection when suddenly I had a brainwave. I bought the onion, the mushrooms, the bacon and the wine and then dashed across the road to the only other place that was still open, KFC. Armed with a Mega Bucket I ran back to mine. I had about 20 minutes to turn these ingredients into something edible that didn't smell like KFC. I took the chicken outside to avoid stinking the whole house out, ripped the breadcrumbed skins off, then chucked the meat in a pot along with the chopped onion, mushrooms and bacon, poured wine over the lot and stuck it in the oven. I also re-fried the sweaty chips to make them crisp and perky again. My *coq au vin et frites* for two did the trick as well: I was with Tana for three weeks until she got fed up with the hours I was working and dumped me.

The real romantic high point of Chewton Glen came as the result of a last-minute, two-week self-catering holiday to Tenerife that I got cheap off Teletext. The holiday came with a hired scooter and a massive apartment that would have been big enough for four. Unfortunately I was still up to my eyes in debt and, unbeknown to me, booking the holiday had maxed out my credit card. When I tried to fill up the tank of the scooter my card was declined and that was it, an entire fortnight's holiday with no scooter, no food and nothing to do. At the time I was a little bit on the fat side. Since I'd been at Chewton Glen, I'd taken to eating about two dozen *pains au chocolat* for breakfast every day. With hardly any money, though, I spent those two weeks in Tenerife eating nothing but fruit from the market and walking everywhere, and when I returned I was a tanned shadow of my former self.

I'd been back less than a week when the new thin me landed a stunning new girlfriend. I was sitting in the staff canteen on my lunch break trying to convince my mates to come with me to the cinema to see the new Bond film, but no one was interested; either that or they all had plans. Anyway, having been knocked back by all my friends a voice piped up from the table behind me: 'I'll come with you.' I turned round and sitting there was the tanned, hair-tied-back stunner with the considerable assets who'd caused me to make such an undignified entrance in the car park on my first day. Slightly embarrassed, I told her that it was all right, she didn't have to, I wasn't looking for a sympathy vote. She said, 'It's not sympathy. I'd really like to.'

She and I were together for about a year and a half after that.

I was really happy at Chewton Glen. The work was good, I had a life again, a newish car, a beautiful girlfriend, and while I wasn't raking it in and I hadn't actually cleared any of my debts, they weren't getting any bigger, which all things considered was a bonus. But I've never liked sitting still or getting complacent, and when the hotel manager asked me to be sous chef at a new hotel he was opening in Winchester with Chewton Glen's head wine waiter Gerard Basset, I jumped at the chance.

The Hotel Du Vin was one of the first of the new breed of boutique hotels. The bistro, which looked more or less identical to One Ninety Queen's Gate, was meant to be a shop window for the hotel, and Gerard, who was one of the most respected sommeliers in the world, was a key selling point – hence the name Hotel du Vin. It was a shame that me and Gerard didn't really get on that well at the time. I respected him, but it was a case of two talented people who don't meet in the middle. It wasn't a good place to be when me and him were in a room together. Still, it was an opportunity too good to pass up, and although it meant leaving Chewton Glen, it was a promotion and a golden chance to be involved with something from the start.

There were five candidates who auditioned for the position of head chef of the Hotel Du Vin. They came at two-hourly intervals into the kitchen at Chewton Glen, were given a selection of ingredients – scallops, black pudding, veal, venison and some other bits – and told to cook any dish they liked, which was then sampled by the managers and the chef of Chewton Glen. As future sous chef of the Hotel Du Vin I helped the candidates out, showing them where everything was and getting them anything they needed.

After a whole day of this, the managers retired to the office where a lot of head scratching went on. Then I was called in. They couldn't decide between the five and wanted to know what I thought. I said that I thought the second one was all right. One of the interviewers disagreed. He'd done some digging and found out that chef number two had a reputation as an arse. There was a moment of exhausted silence, then he asked me, 'Why don't you cook something?' The other two basically shrugged and said, 'Why not?' so off I went. I thought I'd keep it nice and simple so I did a little scallop and black pudding salad with celeriac mash and pea shoots. Truth be told, I wasn't really taking it that seriously. It was just a bit of fun. After all, I already had a job lined up. All the other chefs had taken an hour and a half to do their dishes; mine took 15 minutes.

I delivered my dish and went back into the kitchen to finish clearing down. After more huddled conversation, they came out of the office and said, 'We'll be honest with you, that was better than anything we've eaten all day, and we think you're the man for the job. So how about it? Do you want to be head chef?'

Put it this way, I didn't have to be asked twice.

I was a few weeks short of my 22nd birthday and I was head chef of the Hotel Du Vin. Of course, stupidly, I didn't ask for any more money. I'd been offered eleven grand to be sous chef and no better offers were put on the table to match the new job title. Everyone else they'd seen that day would have been on at least 30 grand, so I was a bargain. In fact I was probably the least well-paid chef in the country. But that didn't matter. I was about to get my own kitchen, my own team and a blank menu to fill. I was about to achieve one of my biggest ambitions eight years early. I was about to be a head chef.

13 THE CAR-FANATIC FATHER I NEVER HAD

My mum never really seemed interested in cars, not when I was growing up. She either drove my dad's – the Audis, the Fords and the French things – or she drove the 'bargains' he bought for her, like her clapped-out Beetle. The most exciting car I remember her having was a red MkII Fiesta XR2 that my dad had treated her to for a birthday or something. It wasn't a new one and he probably got a deal on it, but it was by far the coolest car we ever had.

I remember my cousin, who was very successful, came round once in her brand-new Toyota MR2, white with a blue interior. My mother came running into the lounge yelling, 'James, James, James, you've got to look at this car, you've got to look at this car!' I don't think I have seen her that excitable except for the time we locked her out of the house as a joke when we were little kids, pulling faces at the windows as she went from door to door trying to get through. We thought it was great fun, that is until Mum got one of those wooden clothes drying things from the garden and, like an act from Camelot, raced down the front pathway towards the glass front door with her 10 foot wooden lance. Crash! The glass was gone, we shouted, 'What have you done?!' She got the door open though.

My cousin's MR2 was down at the bottom of the same pathway, all white and gleaming, and me and Mum sat inside together. This was before I'd sat in my first Ferrari – the 308 in the garage at Castle Howard – so this to me was a pretty mega car. I sat in it for ages, twiddling all the knobs and flicking the switches. It's the only time during my childhood I can remember my mum getting really excited about a car, but then we lived in a quiet little village so there wasn't much of anything to get excited about.

I've always been close with my mum, but my parents split up when I was 21. When Mum left she said to me, 'I know you hate me now for this, but give it two months and you'll see why.' I told her I didn't hate her because I knew it was my dad who was mostly to blame. I'd known things weren't great between my parents for a while. A separation had been on the cards for a long time because my dad had been a bit of a nightmare. My mum had only stuck at it for the sake of me and my sister; she said she wanted to be there for us. Once both of us had left it was time for her to get on with her life. I think this was her time – her time to be herself and to live the life she always wanted, which she only felt able to do once the kids had flown the nest.

My mum's boss Pete was, and is, a great guy and a real

car nut, and after my parents divorced he became her fella. I'd known him all through my teens and he probably had the biggest influence on me in terms of my passion for motors. The very first car of his that I remember was a black Ford Fiesta XR2. Fantastic.

In every respect he was the exact opposite of my father. He was always buying new cars, and like the black XR2, he always bought *the* car with all the right bits on it. Where my dad, after looking at a Ford Orion, would go for the 1.4 litre, Pete would get the 1.6 injection Ghia, the proper one that everybody wanted, with the nice alloys and the body kit. Pete had some great cars. For a while he was a Ford fanatic. He had Orions and Sapphires, but they wouldn't be just any old Sapphires, they'd be white ones with skirts and spoilers (this is back when white was really, really cool on a car and skirts and spoilers were a must-have). Like me, he would never be happy with just the standard model; he'd always have to trick it with a body kit or extras. Then he had a Toyota Supra, again white, with black interior, and bloody quick. That was followed by the car everybody wanted: the Escort RS Turbo, the white one with blue writing down the side. Nothing came close to that car. That was definitely cool (well ... at the time). After that, and after a lifetime of being Ford mad, he made a strange detour and bought a Mercedes-Benz 250 which he hated and didn't keep. That's when my mum convinced him to test-drive an Audi. Despite the dreadful colour choices, my mum had really enjoyed driving my dad's Audi 80 and Audi 100. Pete fell in love with the marque and is now on his fourth TT. The TT has a bit too much of the cut'n'blowdry to it for my tastes, but it suits his lifestyle and is perfect for him and my mum to whizz around in. And to be honest, if Pete likes it, it must be good.

A photographer by trade, Pete used to mix his passions, taking photographs of the RAC Rally in the Dalby Forest in the seventies and eighties. He was even a rally navigator for a while. For years before they got together, my mum was his secretary; she used to run the office and his studio in the centre of Malton. I was eleven when she first went to work for him so most of my formative years were spent around Pete and his passion. Some of it was bound to rub off. My mum used to do these dinner parties at our house and Pete used to park his latest new car in the farmyard round the back. I'd grab the keys off him and sit in the driver's seat, pushing the buttons all evening while the grown-ups were having dinner. The first time I ever saw electric windows was in one of Pete's cars. Our car just had the ordinary old-fashioned winders. I sat there all night pressing the button to make the windows go up and down. It's a wonder the battery wasn't flat at the end of the night. I was so amazed by them. I just remember thinking how ace these windows were; like something from another planet. There was nothing cooler, except maybe for the electric wing mirrors, which were almost too amazing for me to comprehend. CD players, electric seats, an electric sunroof – the first time I saw any of these things was in cars owned by Pete.

The other thing I remember vividly is that Pete's cars were all in mint condition. Marks, nicks, scratches … his motors never had any. They were always pristine. Most people say that a car is the second most expensive thing you'll ever own after your house, but it's the thing they don't look after; they just accept dings and dents as normal wear and tear. I can't. I can't stand looking at them, it does my head in, and I'm sure I got that from Pete and his immaculate motors. I always wished my dad would have cars like that, but I knew he never would. Pete didn't have any kids so he obviously had different priorities; he was doing well at work and didn't have any family commitments. Still, my dad could probably have afforded a better car than any he had, he just chose not to. It just wasn't his thing. It's not really surprising that I ended up getting on better with Pete than I did with my own father.

When we were young, my sister and I would go to Pete's studio to see Mum after school and at lunchtime. We'd eat our sandwiches and make a mess of the place, cluttering it up with our bags and rubbish, but Pete was always very good to us. I was interested in his work so he'd take me off to one side and show me stuff – how to mount pictures, how to frame them – and he treated me like the son he didn't have. He was always very supportive, and always very proud of me. I don't know if Pete's more proud of me now than my father is. It's hard to tell because my dad's almost never been outwardly emotional with me or anyone else. But Pete has seen what I've done, seen me come from nothing to achieve success, and I know he's proud of me for that. With my father, it's harder to say. I think, though, that deep down part of him is.

When Pete arrived on the scene with his amazing, hi-tech, top-spec motors it was inevitable we were going to get on. Cars may have been our first connection, but there was also an emotional bond that never existed with my dad. Today I talk to Pete more than I speak to my father. I'll speak to my dad for probably half an hour a month on the phone; I'll speak to Pete for maybe half an hour every day. We'll talk about cars, photography, anything and everything. If I wanted advice about work or a business deal or a relationship, anything that required a bit of worldly wisdom and a trustworthy opinion, it would be Pete I'd call. And while Pete treated me like the son he'd never had, he was also the dad I'd always wanted. Life's very black and white to my father, and sometimes you're not after just a 'yes' or 'no' answer. Sometimes you're looking for conversation, to discuss options, to ponder things. My dad would never do that. It's black or it's white, and that's that. I'm not blaming him for the way he is, but sometimes you don't want to fight every battle on your own or learn things the hard way, character building though it might be.

I was happy when Mum and Pete got together. They're a fantastic couple, they get on brilliantly, they're soul mates and best friends. They're incredibly happy together, and I'm pleased that they found each other. Unfortunately, not everyone in our family felt the same way. When couples split, people take sides, including the children. While I definitely blamed my father for the problems in my parents' marriage, for my sister it was the other way round. My dad and Charlotte had always been very close, the classic father-daughter thing, and when my mum left it was obvious my sister was going to side with my dad. They went one way, me and my mum went the other. With my sister, like my dad, everything's black and white; there's no grey or middle ground. In her mind, mum had left, so she was to blame and my dad was the injured party. This of course guaranteed that every phone call between me and my sister ended in an argument. It was a terrible time, both the highest and lowest point of my life. On the one hand I was just months away from realising a dream and being made head chef at the Hotel Du Vin; on the other hand my family had just imploded and my sister and I had fallen out big time. Thankfully, the rift between me and Charlotte was short-lived, but in order for things between us to improve, things between me and my dad had literally to hit a new low. One night not long before I left Chewton Glen for the Hotel Du Vin, the head chef called me into his office just before the start of evening service. It was a Friday night about half six and chef was sitting there at his desk with the phone in his hand. He said that my sister was on the phone and I should know she was in tears. I thought something terrible had happened, that someone had had an accident, so I prepared myself for the worst and took the receiver. I couldn't actually understand what she was saying at first, she was crying so hard. I just about got her to calm down, and she told me that she was at our house, that she was sitting in one of the old pig sheds and that some of our stuff from the house was out there in plastic bin liners. She was in a terrible state so I told her to stay there, I was on my way. I jumped into my little Fiesta and drove like a lunatic all the way up to Yorkshire. I drove five hours straight, didn't stop, just kept going and going. As much as we weren't getting on at the time, she sounded so low that I knew I had to get to her as soon as possible, so apart from filling up with petrol I just gunned it all the way there. When I arrived, at about eleven at night, she was still in the pig shed with the bin bags. Our old bedrooms were being remodelled and next thing we knew our stuff was in bin bags outside in the shed.

I'd started to help Charlotte when my dad drove into the yard in his Peugeot 405. He got out of the car and came storming through the shed, shouting, wanting to know what we were doing at his house. 'You no longer live here, you're no longer welcome,' he barked. My sister was going nuts, crying and wailing, so I told him to calm down, we weren't stopping, we'd just sort through the stuff and then go.

I'll never forgive my father for that night, for making us feel so unwanted. Never. Things have never been the same between us since. They probably never will be either. A heart can only take so many stones thrown at it before it stops beating. And over the years both my sister and I have had to put up with a lot, but this was it for me. My sister and I buried our differences on the spot, and me and my dad didn't speak again for two years.

But like I said, my mum was and always will be there for me and has been a huge influence on my life. I will always be grateful for her love and how she's cared for me, and same goes for my gran. When I was little I spent hours in the kitchen watching her cook (while granddad got upset when whatever old horse he had bet on came in last again. Had to love him for trying though). So, I'd sit there in gran's kitchen at the old table watching *Come Dancing*, while she would rub butter and flour together in a worn out bowl for the next batch of biscuits, which always seemed to be in the oven. Gran was one of the greatest people in the world, and amongst many things I can safely say she made the best bacon sandwiches ever, which were the perfect cure for every hurt. I know this isn't a cookbook, but here's the recipe for Gran's Best Bacon Sarnies:

1. *Take one gran and one auntie on a Thursday (pension day)*
2. *Take the bus to M&S and head for the bread section, and with bums in the air and stocking tops showing, squeeze every loaf of bread at the back of the shelf to find the most in-date and softest loaf of thin-sliced*
3. *Visit Scott's Butchers in York on the way back home for a pound of smoked best back bacon*
4. *Turn on the gas grill on the old enamel cooker, place the bacon under the flames*
5. *Meanwhile, butter the bread so much it comes through to the other side*
5. *Place the cooked bacon on top of the buttered bread, press with old granny hands (this is the secret ingredient), cut in half, put onto your very best china and serve to one hungry kid*

The only problem was that it would take her so long to make them and me so little time to eat them. I still can't make them like she did, but even so, they always make me feel better.

14 *HOW A KIT CAR SAVED MY LIFE: THE WESTFIELD, PART I*

I could have accidentally ended up living a life of unimaginable boredom, a suburban nightmare of tidy front gardens with neat little flower beds and gnomes, a double garage with plenty of room for the kids' bikes and a nice Ford Mondeo estate parked outside. I could have had all this if I hadn't bought my two-seater open-top sports car. It was a close call.

I'd been head chef at the Hotel Du Vin in Winchester for nine months when I decided it was time for a new car. So I sold my little 1.9 Fiesta Diesel through *AutoTrader* for just over a grand, which was a hell of a lot of money to me in those days. With the Fiesta gone, I was in the market for something a little more exciting, especially as every day Chris, my sous chef, and I would sit on the wall outside during our breaks and watch a steady stream of amazing cars flowing into the hotel car park.

I first met Pippa, who became a good mate and later my PA, because she used to leave her Porsche 911 Carrera 4, white with blue interior, in the car park while she and her boyfriend Steve went drinking in Winchester. We only met because Chris and I, working every hour God sent, used to see Pippa come and pick it up again in the morning. It seemed like everyone had a great car, and with a grand in my pocket I had ambitions of getting something just as cool, if not quite as expensive. And that turned out to be a Westfield kit car.

This was 1995. At the time I was sharing a flat with Chris above Chinese and Indian takeaways. My room was over the Chinese; Chris's was over the Indian. We didn't have a garage. My basic salary for two weeks was £326. After rent, council tax, income tax and national insurance, my take-home pay for a fortnight was £183, or £91.50 a week. The good news was that though my take-home was nearly non-existent, I was back to working the same 18-hour days I'd been doing at One Ninety Queen's Gate, so I didn't have time to spend any of it.

One night after service I was in the flat watching late-night TV when an advert came on for a loan company ('Are you looking to buy a new car?'). I was still about eleven grand in debt from my time in London, but I thought, 'Sod it.' I made a note of the number and the next morning I gave them a call. After crunching some numbers they said that they could lend me £8,000. I went straight out to the newsagent's, bought a copy of *AutoTrader*, flicked through the pages, and there it was: Westfield SE, blue, 1,500 miles, cycle wings, K&N Alloys, K&N Filters, 2 litre Ford Pinto engine, Lucas Harness, £8,000.

One of the waitresses from the hotel kindly offered to give me a lift to go and see it. We drove down this little quiet suburban street, me with £8,000 in cash in my bag, found the right house, and I rang the doorbell. A guy came out, opened the garage door, and there it was, this absolutely immaculate dark-blue sports car. It was almost exactly the same as the Caterham 7, only it had a slightly longer wheel base and was wider, which made it perfect for someone of my height. It was awesome. A very smart little car. As soon as he opened the garage door it was sold, but being a Yorkshireman I tried to have a little haggle. I offered him £7,500. Once he'd finished telling me where the door was I offered him £7,750 and a free meal at the Hotel Du Vin, which he accepted (I told him to complain about the food first, which was the only way I'd be able to sort him out with a complimentary meal). He came to the restaurant about four weeks later.

So now I was almost 20 grand in debt, but I had myself a proper little sports car and I was as happy as could be. Understandably I wanted to share my joy and excitement, so the following weekend I drove over to the New Forest to see my girlfriend. We were having a semi-long-distance relationship. She had her job at Chewton Glen and didn't want to move to Winchester, so it was a case of seeing each other when we could, which with the hours I was working wasn't often. When I got there she took one look at my new toy and said, 'What do you want that for? It's ridiculous.' She didn't really appreciate it and I couldn't be bothered to try to convince her, so we went for a walk instead, leaving the Westfield parked on the drive of her parents' house.

Her father was retired and lived in a stereotypical Barratt home. On their estate the houses came in two-, four- and six-bedroom variants, and they had a six-bedroom one with a double garage, which meant he was doing all right. When we got back from our walk, she and I walked up the path, past the perfectly planted front garden, through the front door and into the lounge.

It was like walking into an interview. Sat there on the sofa was her brother and his wife – both supermarket managers and about to have their first kid – along with her mum, and her dad. My girlfriend sat down next to her mum on the sofa, and her dad invited me to take a seat on this chair that was all on its own right in the middle of the room.

'I think we ought to have a chat,' he said.

All of a sudden her brother started up. 'You need to look to your future,' he advised. 'You need to be thinking about buying a house, not ridiculous cars like that one out there.'

I was thinking, 'Hold on a minute, what's this got to do with you?'

Her dad then said, 'Have you got financial planning?'

'No,' I said, thinking it was probably best not to mention that what I did have was a mountain of debt.

'Right, well, we need to think about this,' he continued. 'You're going out with my daughter and you're going to get engaged in the next year or so ...'

My girlfriend was nodding along with all this. Then her mother started.

After about two hours I got up and said, 'Sorry, I can't listen to this any more,' and I walked out. My girlfriend was in tears, and while her mother comforted her, her dad followed me out with the brother and started lecturing me – 'You need to be a man and we need to talk about this situation' – while I was getting in the car and strapping myself into the seatbelts (full Lucas racing harnesses). I fired it up, stuck it into first and put my foot on the accelerator. The wheels spun, the back went sideways, the front swung out to the right, and instead of pulling out of their driveway I went straight across the flower bed, churned up all the flowers and turned their perfect front garden into a bomb site. With that I was gone off up the road, never to be seen again.

I returned to Winchester a free man in my trusty Westfield. If it was a toss-up between the missus and the Westfield, I was always going home a single man. If her dad didn't know it beforehand he'd certainly grasped by now that the one thing I didn't want was a nice normal life with 2.4 kids and no hope of anything more exciting than a round of golf to look forward to. It's not that I wanted money and all the trappings of success, I was always just after an interesting life. I wanted more than the Monday-to-Friday nine-to-five, getting pissed on a Friday night, going shopping with the missus on the Saturday, spending Sunday afternoon watching TV, and then starting it all over again. I couldn't do that. If I'd wanted that I'd have done what most of my mates did and gone and worked in Malton bacon factory straight after school. After all, most of them were earning more money than I was when I was working at One Ninety Queen's Gate and it didn't nearly half kill them in the process. But I didn't want that. I wanted something different. So I'm grateful to her dad because, really, he did me a favour.

15 SCREEN TESTS: THE WESTFIELD, PART II

I went everywhere and did everything in the Westfield, which was fine when that meant blatting round the place for the fun of it. Then, having a two-seater with no roof or boot to speak of was fine. Who needed a boot or a roof when you were driving through the New Forest late at night to unwind after a manic night's service, or hoofing it with Chris to the Ministry of Sound in London to dance on podiums like nutters until the small hours of Saturday morning? When I first started to do TV, though, finding somewhere for all my pots and pans, never mind the ingredients, was a challenge. You've never seen a passenger seat and footwell so crammed. The lack of a roof and proper heating caused problems too. At one stage, when I was doing a spot on *The Big Breakfast*, I had 5.30 am call times, and that wasn't much fun in the winter. I used to leave home at 3.30 am, freezing cold, my teeth chattering and my pans rattling next to me, drive from Winchester to East London, do my cooking with Chris Evans and Gaby Roslin, get back in the Westfield and be back in Winchester at the Hotel Du Vin by 11.30 ready to cook lunch for 60.

The brigade at the Hotel Du Vin was so small that initially there was never any question of taking time off to do anything like TV. We were working six days a week as it was and only just managing to pull through. In fact, we were so stretched and busy that my big break in TV almost didn't happen.

As I said, there was an eight-week wait for a table and one Saturday night Loyd Grossman came in without a reservation. I suggested to the head waiter that he sit him and his companion at the bar and I'd knock them up a risotto and a pudding. Towards the end of the evening I went through to the bar where Loyd and his friend were finishing their meal. It had been a crazy service, we were all completely exhausted and I'd gone to get four beers for the guys in the kitchen who had more than earned a drink. As I was getting them the bar manager said, 'I'll charge you for those.' That was it. I turned round and in front of Loyd, his companion and everyone else I told the bar manager to 'shove it up your fucking arse'.

As I walked off, Loyd's companion stopped me and introduced herself as Chantal Rutherford Browne. She was a TV producer, and she was looking for chefs for a new programme Sky were doing. I said thanks but no thanks, but she gave me her card and told me to call her if I changed my mind. I went back to the kitchen, told everyone that this woman with Loyd Grossman had just tried to chat me up, and thought nothing more of it.

A week later Chantal called to see if I'd changed my mind. As it happened I'd just had a very shit day in the kitchen, and I thought, 'Why not?' I told her I had next Tuesday off; what did she want me to do?

I went up to London to do a screen test – Chantal paid for my train ticket because I was so broke I couldn't afford it – and a couple of weeks later she got back in touch to say that everyone was really impressed with me and they wanted me to do a regular cooking slot for this live magazine programme for Sky One called *Sky One to Three*. They wanted me to do it once a week, which I said was OK, because I only had one day a week off. She asked what my fee would be. I said I didn't know; what was she offering? She said that their standard fee was £300. I thought £300 a month sounded amazing (remember, I was on £91.50 take-home a week). When she said they'd cover all my expenses as well I told her it was a deal.

My slot was two and a half minutes. The first week I was on the guests were the Bee Gees. The second week it was Kylie Minogue. It was unreal. I was on live TV with Kylie Minogue. After three weeks Chantal called to tell me that my slot was the most popular item on the programme and they wanted me to do two a week. I said, 'No way. I'm working my nuts off as it is, we're down staff at work, and there's no way I can get any more time off.' She said they could pre-record one of the slots so I could do them both on the same day if that helped. Well, they were paying me £300 a month and I wanted to keep them sweet, so I agreed, and that's what we did.

Not long after that my first cheque came through. I was straight on the phone to Chantal.

'I think there's been a mistake,' I told her. 'I thought we agreed £300. I've got a cheque here for £1,800.'

There was a pause, then Chantal said, 'Yes, that's right.'

'It's not right,' I said.

'You've done six slots so far at £300 a slot,' she reasoned, 'that's £1,800.'

I'd done 15 minutes' worth of cooking and I'd just been paid what it would take me two months to earn at the Hotel Du Vin. Suddenly television seemed like the best thing ever.

I did *Sky One to Three* for about three months, driving up to London every week with the passenger seat and footwell of the Westfield overflowing. Then, just as suddenly as it had started, the phone stopped ringing. Obviously I was disappointed, but I thought, 'Well, that's it, my 15 minutes of fame are up, and I was paid bloody well for them.' All the boys at work were taking the piss out of me a bit, but I'd had worse.

Two months down the line, it was a busy Friday night and the kitchen phone rang. I hated the phone ringing when I was in the middle of service so I let Chris get it. The woman on the other end asked for me. Chris told her I was a bit busy at the moment, but the woman was very insistent.

'Chef, she really wants to speak to you,' Chris said.

'Well you can tell whoever it is to fuck off,' I replied. 'I'm in the middle of fucking service.'

Just to hammer home the point, I walked over, grabbed

the phone out of Chris's hand and slammed the receiver down.

It rang again. This time I picked it up, shouted 'Will you fuck off!' down it and slammed it down again. This happened another couple of times, so I jumped across the hot plate, stormed into reception and told the poor girl on the desk to stop putting these bloody calls through, didn't she know we were busy?

At about 10.30 the phone rang again. Now, generally, if the phone rang at that time of night it was a supplier, so I answered this time and this female voice said, 'Hello, this is Mary, can I speak to James Martin?'

'Yeah, speaking,' I said.

'Oh good,' she said. 'This is *Ready Steady Cook*. Now fuck off.' And she slammed the phone down.

Ready Steady Cook was the biggest cooking show on television. A call from them was a very big deal indeed. I checked that it wasn't one of the commis chefs mucking about, then kicked myself for not finding out who it was before telling them to fuck off. Luckily, at nine the next morning Mary phoned back and said that, seriously, she was from *Ready Steady Cook* and they'd really like me to do a screen test. So my next day off was spent at Television Centre in Wood Lane. The BBC sent a chauffeur-driven Mercedes, blacked-out windows and all, to pick me up and the driver was giggling to himself because, as usual, I was in the back pressing all the buttons like a kid. I did the audition, which involved making up a dish from a carrier bag of random ingredients (just like the programme) while a panel of six people threw questions at me, then when I was done I decided to go for a walk down Wood Lane, all the way to Shepherd's Bush, to cool down.

As I was walking down the road my phone rang. It was my mother, wanting to know how it went. She was full of motherly wisdom about how if I didn't get it at least I knew I'd done my best. I thanked her for the vote of confidence, and as I hung up the phone rang again. It was Mary.

'Do you have an agent?' she asked me.

Through Castle Howard, my dad knew Les Dawson and Richard Whiteley. He gave them a call to ask if they could recommend an agent for me. I was put in touch with John Wilcox, whose speciality was newsreaders and presenters. He agreed to take me on and sorted everything out with the BBC, and with that I was a chef on *Ready Steady Cook*, earning the same as Ainsley Harriott, Brian Turner and my old boss Antony Worrall Thompson.

I'd been on the show a couple of months and things were getting busier when John Wilcox said that really I needed an agent more suited to what I was doing. Antony put me in touch with his agent, Fiona Lindsay, and from then on everything went totally nuts. Suddenly I was doing photo shoots for *Company* magazine for their '50 Most Eligible Bachelors' feature, and getting six sackfuls of mail delivered to the restaurant from women who felt they could be the one to make me give up my bachelor status. (Little did I know that some of the kitchen and waiting staff thought it would be funny to reply on my behalf asking for more photos, maybe something in a bikini. They, or I, got replies too!)

With *Ready Steady Cook*, the *Company* magazine article, *The Big Breakfast* and the *Ready Steady Cook* magazine (for which I was writing a regular column – which meant two trips to the computer shop in the Westfield because I couldn't get the computer and the monitor on the passenger seat at the same time), my profile was very quickly going through the roof. The bigger it got, the more work Fiona was able to get for me, and the less my bosses at the Hotel Du Vin liked it. My mum told me not to make any rash decisions; for all I knew the TV work could be short-lived and I shouldn't throw in the day job just yet. My dad agreed, and so did I, so I stuck at it, just about managing to keep everything afloat. I never let the restaurant or Chris and the rest of the brigade down. My work never suffered.

Still, one day the manager of the Hotel Du Vin called me into the office and said that I had a choice to make: it was the hotel or TV, and if I knew what was good for me I'd choose the hotel. The problem, it seemed, was that my profile was bigger than the restaurant's, and he wasn't happy about that. The only other option was for me to let him run my TV career, which I could have told him there and then was never going to happen. He told me to go away and think about where my heart lay.

I went away, I thought, and I decided that my heart lay in my wallet and my career, not in his. My decision to leave came as quite a shock to him, and he then decided that I'd leave when he said, not when I wanted to. He told me I could only go once they'd found a suitable replacement, not before. Between Chewton Glen and the Hotel Du Vin

I'd worked for this guy for about five years. I'd given him everything. I'd worked stupid hours for crap money and never asked for more. I'd worked six months without a day off when the Hotel Du Vin first opened and I'd hardly ever complained. So I couldn't believe this. I remember walking up the stairs from the office and being absolutely furious. I could have walked there and then, but I decided to bide my time. After all, that weekend it was his birthday, and on the Saturday night he had 60 people coming for dinner.

As the week wore on I didn't say anything more about the conversation we'd had, or about leaving, I just went about my work as usual. Then on Saturday evening I walked up to the manager, said thanks very much for everything, got in my little Westfield and drove off into the sunset. It wasn't big or clever, but it felt good, and I thought he deserved it.

Actually, I should have been thanking him. I should have been cooking him something extra special to thank him for doing for me pretty much what my ex-girlfriend's dad had done: forcing me to make a decision I needed to make but probably never would have done on my own. I could have gone on for years trying to balance a misplaced loyalty and my ever-growing workload. As it was, Fiona was starting to have to turn down offers because I could only get one day a week off, so leaving the hotel was the best thing I did. With my diary free, Fiona went into overdrive lining up TV work, demos, appearances, book deals, endorsements, catering gigs and magazine columns. Within a short space of time I went from earning £11 grand a year to bringing in £5 grand a month. I went from not being able to get anyone to give me a mortgage to buying my own flat on Winchester High Street.

More importantly, I went from sitting on the wall outside the Hotel Du Vin drooling over somebody else's Ferrari to driving my own.

16 TRACK DAYS

Cars are a great leveller. A passion for driving and motors can bring together the most unlikely collection of characters and unite people across every imaginable social and economic divide. Which is how I, an overworked, under-paid chef who couldn't even afford to buy a round of drinks let alone anything more exciting than a metallic-green Ford Fiesta 1.9 Diesel (another one I'd bought), came to be best mates with a yacht builder.

I first met Harvey Jones, who runs a big yachting company in Southampton, at the Hotel Du Vin, where he and his mate Alex Edwards used to come. At the time I had no idea what either of them did but I knew they were both quite well to do; more importantly, I knew Harvey was seriously into cars. Alex, who later became a partner in my deli in Winchester because it was next to his clothes shop on the high street, is a very eccentric man who used to drive a blue Vauxhall Cavalier called Bluebell with rust patches so big you had to rest your feet on a plank of wood otherwise they'd go right through the passenger footwell, so there was never any danger of him getting mistaken for a car nut. But Harvey was a proper enthusiast. He used to organise days at Goodwood where he'd hire the track for an afternoon and get together 30 of his mates who'd pay £600 each to blat it round in their cars. The closest Alex had come to a track day was when we used to race each other down the hill on wheelie bins after a night in the pub.

I used to chat to Harvey and Alex when they came into the restaurant and they would take me to their local, the Wickham Arms, where they had late-night lock-ins. I'd go there after service, still in my chef's whites, but I was so broke I could never afford a drink. I used to just sit there, wait until someone else went to the bar and say, 'Yeah, I'll have a pint, thanks.' I'd do that until it was my turn to buy a round – which was about £8 in those days and more than I could run to – then I'd make my excuses and leave, saying I had to get back to the kitchen to finish up. I'd become that guy who never gets a round in. I wanted to, I just didn't have the money in my pocket to do it. After a while Harvey clocked what was happening, that I always left just as it got to my turn to go to the bar. He never said anything about it, but once he'd spotted what was going on he covered for me: whenever it was my round Harvey would step in and say, 'I'll get them.'

Whenever we got together we always talked about cars: what we liked, what we didn't, what was good, what was rubbish, what was coming out, what we'd have if money were no object. Harvey talked a lot about the track days. I'd ask questions, he'd tell me about his latest exploits, and eventually he started inviting me along. He knew there was no way I could ever afford to pay to drive round the track myself, and the diesel Fiesta I had when I first met them wasn't really up to it either, so he used to let me sit in with him as a passenger as he hoofed it around the track in his Escort Cosworth. It was just the best thing. When I got my Westfield, which was pretty much designed as a track car, Harvey asked me if I wanted to bring it along and actually have a go myself. Again, he never charged me.

At the track we'd see every kind of supercar imaginable – GT2 Porsches, Ferraris – and I arrived in my humble eight-grand Westfield wearing a helmet I'd borrowed from Harvey. I watched everyone else going round for a bit, then Harvey came over and said, 'Go on, have a go. See what you think. Just watch the kink in the road on the right and you'll be fine.' So off I went.

I couldn't believe it. I was driving my Westfield around Goodwood! It felt fantastic. The third lap's your flying lap, so I gunned it down the straight, turned right, hit the kink in the road and spun. I did a proper pirouette. I pulled it back to the pits, got out, and the entire car was covered in grass and crap. If I'd gone off left I'd have hit the grass bank and totalled the car, so I was lucky. I was a fish out of water with these people, but it was great, and I was loving it.

After that mishap I really took a look around at all the incredible cars there. 'This is amazing,' I thought. 'If I work hard enough, I could be part of this, I could really belong to it.' Meeting people like that and having those experiences certainly gave you a taste of the good life. From then on my goals in life were based on four wheels. Most people might aspire to a second home or something like that. I don't want a second home, I've only ever wanted cars.

Fast forward a couple of years, and my agent Fiona has just pulled in a couple of really big deals for me. I got a call from her one day inviting me to a party at her flat near Regent's Park. She was very excited, and told me she'd got some big news but couldn't tell me what it was over the phone. When I got there she took me to one side, handed me a cheque for £22,000 and told me that was the first of four payments from Somerfield. All I had to do was a couple of bits of promo and a few demos outside some of the stores. At this time I was still working at the Hotel Du Vin on £11,000 a year, I was over 30 grand in debt, and there I was holding a cheque for £22,000, the first of four. At almost exactly the same time, Fiona landed me my first book deal. Within days of signing with Somerfield I was banking the advance, another cheque for £22,000. Obviously, most people would have done the sensible thing and cleared their debts, and to be fair I did put some aside to bring the balance down a bit. With the rest of it, though, I chose a far more exciting option: I went straight out and bought a Caterham 7.

The Caterham 7 was the two-seater track car my Westfield was based on. Bizarrely, it was actually smaller than the Westfield. Not only was it better suited to a six-footer like me, the Westfield was also far more reliable; Ainsley Harriott and Brian Turner regularly had to give me a push start in the Caterham outside the *Ready Steady Cook* studio, and Chris, my sous chef at the Hotel Du Vin, was forever towing me to the garage, which used to piss him off no end. Needless to say, I didn't keep the Caterham very long, although probably longer than Fiona would have liked.

I used that car every day to go to *Ready Steady Cook* and backwards and forwards to Islington in North London to shoot the photographs for the book *Eating In with James Martin*. These days, because all the marketing begins so far in advance, you shoot the cover of a book first and then you do all the pictures of the food to go inside. A decade ago, though, it was the other way round: I was going up to Islington in the Caterham, getting the food together and photographing it, and the cover was going to be done at the very last minute.

The day before the cover shoot I had a track day at Goodwood. Wild horses couldn't have kept me away from it. It had been a while since the last one and it was my first with the Caterham. I couldn't wait. In the Westfield it had been incredible; in this thing it promised to be eye-popping.

I got up to Goodwood nice and early, got suited up, helmet on, and off I went, driving it round. On the third lap, the flying lap, I gunned it down the straight, turned right, hit the kink in the road, managed not to spin it this time, but instead got clipped on the back by a Morgan next to me and went flying off the track into a straw bale. I just remember my head really, really hurting. Luckily, because I'd hit the bale, there was no damage to the car, but the impact had rocked my head hard and I was convinced I had a serious case of whiplash. I drove back to the pits and Harvey came running over, shouting, 'Are you all right? Are you all right?' I nodded – 'I'm fine, I'm fine' – then I took my helmet off. Harvey's face dropped. 'Oh mate,' he said. 'What? What?' I was saying, but he was just staring in horror, saying 'Oh mate' over and over.

When I looked in the mirror I saw that I'd burst every single blood vessel in my eyes. There was no white left, they were completely red. I called Fiona.

'We've got to move the shoot. My eyes are absolutely screwed. We've got to move it.'

'We can't,' she said. 'We've got no more days. We're on the deadline, the diary's filling up, and by the time your eyes have gone back to normal it'll be too late. We'll just have to get them retouched.'

And that is what we did. On the original edition of *Eating In* they airbrushed the whites of my eyes on all the cover photos, front and back. Unfortunately, airbrushing was pretty crude back then and instead of looking sharp and smart on the front of my very first book it looked like someone had been having a laugh with the Tippex.

17 READY, STEADY ... NOW DON'T DO IT AGAIN: THE LOTUS ELISE, PART I

My first 'proper' car was a Lotus Elise. I'd had other good cars before that, as you know – some dependable Fiestas, the Westfield and Caterham kit cars, other little two-seater open-top things based on the original Lotus 7 sports car – but my first proper car was my Elise. It was stunning. Silver, blue hood, went like anything, a real little pocket rocket.

It was also my first new car. I'd read an article in *Autocar* magazine about this amazing new fibreglass roadster Lotus were going to do. It was 20 grand, which at the time was about two months' wages, so I thought I could afford it, and in the picture it looked like a good bit of kit, so I went down to Westover Cars in Salisbury (which I used to drive past in my Vauxhall Nova when I had nothing) and put a £1,000 deposit down on one. Four months later I went to pick it up and asked them how much they'd give me part-exchange for my green 1.9 Fiesta Diesel with its fake leather steering wheel and 90,000 miles on the clock. Two hundred and fifty quid was all they'd offer me. I'd paid £1,600 for it about six months earlier so I tried to talk them up but they weren't having any of it.

'OK,' I said, 'but I want a stereo in the Elise.'

'Yeah, that's fine,' came the reply, 'except that the hole in the dashboard for the radio is an optional extra.'

'How much?' I asked.

'Two hundred and fifty pounds.'

I loved the Elise though. Drove it everywhere. I did something like 47,000 miles in it, which for a Lotus is unbelievable mileage. But then it was my only car. Having swapped the Fiesta for a hole in the dashboard – yes, the stereo itself was extra – it was my only mode of transport and it took me all over the place doing demos, appearances and TV gigs. It wasn't the most practical everyday car. Again, pots, pans and food had to go on the passenger seat. You couldn't put food in the boot because it was right behind the engine so your salmon would smell of petrol and exhaust fumes and be half cooked by the time you got there. As it was, even if you put the food in the passenger footwell you had to have the air conditioning on full blast to chill it otherwise it would overheat. I managed though. Didn't poison anyone – well, not that I know of. And I didn't want a practical car anyway. I'd done all that with the Fiesta, which did a lot of miles to the gallon, had a big boot and was kind to the environment. And it was boring. I wanted a proper driver's car, and the Lotus was it.

So I had this great car and I wanted to drive it, and the *Ready Steady Cook* tour was just about all the excuse I needed. The show had first aired in 1994 and a few years later the viewing figures were massive, and every one of the 38 dates was a sell-out. It was literally a live version of the TV programme, exactly the same. Fern Britton presented it, a couple of people would come on with their shopping bags and empty them out, and then two chefs – me and Phil Vickery, or Ainsley Harriott and Tony Tobin, or Brian Turner and Antony Worrall Thompson – would do their best to make something edible out of the ingredients. Failing that, I'd just cover everything in spun sugar. I think I held the record for the most consecutive wins on *Ready Steady Cook* with 27, and I owed most of those victories to spun sugar. The only differences with the live shows were that there were four chefs a night – after the interval another two chefs came on and did it all again – and we were doing it in front of several thousand screaming people. They'd go absolutely nuts when we walked on, like nothing else you've ever seen. Crazy. We're talking pop star hysteria.

I did something like 21 of the dates, and I drove to almost all of them in the Elise, which is pretty much how I managed to rack up 47,000 miles in it. Everyone else either went in the tour bus or had cars drive them, but there was no way I was going to be stuck all the time on a tour bus. Where's the fun in sitting on a bus? Buses are for OAPs and the unemployed – no thank you. I had a great car and I wanted to drive it.

That tour went everywhere – London, Reading, Oxford, Manchester, Newcastle – doing a couple of nights in each town. It was a big rock 'n' roll production, and the tour bus was a proper big Rolling Stones type of thing with blacked-out windows, TVs and beds. And practically every night it got trashed. The roadies had all done Status Quo and stuff like that in the past, but I don't think they knew the meaning of rock 'n' roll until they did the *Ready Steady Cook* tour! The programme might have looked all nice and lovely, but when chefs drink, they drink big style, and we were absolutely hammered every night. We had Fairy Liquid fights on that tour bus. We used to put bread on top of other truck drivers' cabs so they'd be woken up at the crack of dawn by birds pecking on the roof. One night I left the driver in agony after he'd pinned me down in a play fight and the only way to get him off was to put Fairy Liquid between my fingers and rub them on his eyes. Not model behaviour, I admit, but then that's chefs for you. The road crew got hit hardcore with some of the stuff we got up to on that tour, but it was our last night in Llandudno when they really found out that when it comes to behaving badly, chefs are a match for any rock band.

For anyone who hasn't been there, Llandudno is a quiet, sleepy Welsh seaside town. It's the Scarborough of Wales, an 'olde worlde' place, full of guest houses and old people on benches along the seafront. There's not exactly a lot to do. It's the kind of place where you have to make your own entertainment, and for a load of bored chefs, beered up and on an adrenalin high after the evening's show, that entertainment is going to involve someone getting into some kind of trouble. Possibly with the police.

So there we were, me and a load of roadies and the *Ready Steady Cook* crew, in this sleepy seaside town, in the car park of the exhibition centre, which is bang in the middle of the seafront, in our big tour bus with blacked-out windows. We all hit the drink, and at about eleven pm some bright spark, probably me, decided to cook a Scooby snack on one of those disposable barbecues. One of the guys whizzed off and got some bacon and sausages, and I was put in charge of cooking them. Then I suddenly had a brainwave. A couple of days earlier I had taken the Elise over to Goodwood for a track day with my old mate Harvey Jones, and I still had my flameproof racing suit in the boot. I decided it would be a great idea to put it on this girl, a member of the *Ready Steady Cook* production crew, lie her on the ground in the middle of the car park and cook the sausages and bacon on the disposable barbecue on her stomach.

Fast forward ten minutes, and I'm stood there in my chef's whites and my bandanna (which I always wore on *Ready Steady Cook*), turning over the sausages and cooking up the bacon, while this poor girl – who, it should be pointed out, had necked just as many beers as the rest of us and was a more than willing participant – is keeping as still as she can, trying to balance the barbecue. Unbeknown to us, the whole thing is being watched by the police on CCTV cameras in the car park. Next minute it's all flashing lights and sirens and the tour manager's locking me in the bus loo. The police give everyone a telling off – 'Don't start campfires in the car park' – and I can hear all the roadies and crew, including the girl in the flameproof suit, who's got these two huge brown marks on her chest and stomach from where the barbecue was resting, being very apologetic and saying that they're sorry, officers, they won't do it again.

Now, you'd think that after such a close call, and having escaped with only a good talking to, we'd think ourselves lucky and call it a night. If anything, though, it just made us bolder. We got more and more pissed, then I decided that the tour bus wanted brightening up a bit, that it could do with a little of the Laurence Llewelyn-Bowen treatment, so I walked over the road to the beautifully maintained seafront, got hold of a palm tree, dragged it out of its pot, back over the road, into the car park, up the steps and on to the bus.

Fast forward another ten minutes, and the police are back in the car park demanding that the missing palm tree is handed over while the tour manager is denying all knowledge, saying that there must be some misunderstanding. This time I'm in the luggage compartment under the bus, hugging the palm tree to my chest. The policeman very politely asks our tour manager to follow him the 150 feet over the road to the empty plant pot and then asks him to look back towards the bus at the mud trail leading all the way to it across the road and the car park. Luckily he's a very nice policeman with a sense of humour and he just tells everyone to calm down and put the palm tree back.

The next morning, with the palm tree back where it belonged, the flameproof suit back in the boot and our human barbecue having suffered no ill effects – the poor thing works on *Big Brother* now, for her sins – I drove back home to Winchester in the Elise and had one of the greatest drives of my life. It was just one of those never-forget-it-as-long-as-you-live experiences. I stayed off the motorways, drove all the way back on the windy roads, through the Welsh mountains and little villages. The sun was shining, I had the hood down, the radio was blasting out, and everything in life was great. I didn't even know where I was going. I just had a rough idea of points to head for and figured that as long as I was going south I'd be all right. I never once looked at the map, I just blasted it and had the best drive. I don't think I've ever enjoyed driving a car as much as I enjoyed driving the Lotus that day. Incredible.

It might have had something to do with the fact that the Elise was my first really big buy after things started to take off for me (obviously, buying somewhere to live came a poor second to a car, always has). Prior to that the most expensive thing I'd treated myself to was a Breitling NaviTimer watch, like the one Tiff Needell used to wear on *Top Gear*. That wasn't the pleasant shopping experience it should have been though. I went with my mum into York to buy it and we literally had two security guards follow us around the shop like they were convinced I was going to nick something. It got to the point where we were so uncomfortable that after trying it on we left and I went and bought exactly the same watch from a shop up the road.

I got the engine supercharged after reading in a magazine about this company near Teddington that specialised in increasing the brake horsepower of Lotus Elises. Mine was a standard 1.8 model, and me and standard are two things that don't really go together. Having 'tricked out' practically every skateboard, BMX, motorbike and car I'd ever owned, the thought of a supercharged Elise was too much to resist. They had three packages: for two grand they'd tweak the engine a bit, get an extra 20bhp out of it; for three and a half grand they'd change the filters and tweak the engine a bit more, another 15bhp; or there was the five grand option which more or less doubled the bhp from the standard 118 to 210 and added two big fat exhaust pipes. I handed over my five grand. It completely wiped me out until the next pay cheque, but it was worth every penny. When it came back, bloody hell, what a car that thing was! Quick? It was lethal. Even by today's standards it would be fast. That thing was just an animal.

I found out just how quick it was one night when I had to hoof it back from Bristol to London in record time because a certain TV actress and lads' mag pin-up had requested the pleasure of my company. I was in Bristol doing a demo for Stellar, a pan company I've been working with for years, and in between demos I was getting text messages from Brian Turner. He was in London filming *Celebrity Ready Steady Cook* and he was keeping me up to date with the scores. We used to do six shows a day and there'd be three chefs doing two shows each, so he was texting things like 'One down, one to go, one-nil'. We'd only just started doing these prime-time celebrity specials so it was all still a big deal, and they were hugely popular and getting amazing viewing figures, so it was a real privilege for both the chefs and the celebrities to be asked to do it. I asked Brian who his next celebrity was, and he came back with 'Lisa Faulkner'. Now Lisa was an actress on TV at the time. She was starring in BBC1's *Holby City* and had just been voted one of *FHM*'s 100 Sexiest Women in the World. I texted Brian back – 'She's a bit of all right' – and then got back to my demo.

About eight o'clock I got a call on my mobile. It was Brian, and he sounded very excited. 'Mate, we're going out for a drink tonight, you've got to come to London,' he said. I was just finishing off, clearing up my bits and pieces and signing a few books and autographs. I wasn't in any particular hurry because I only had to drive back to Winchester, and to be honest, the thought of driving 120 miles to London wasn't really doing it for me. Plus it was a Thursday night. The celebrity shows were normally filmed at the weekend because the audiences were better (younger), but for some reason this was a Thursday. I was tired and I couldn't be bothered, so I said to Brian that if it was all the same to him I think I'd give it a miss. But he was having none of it. 'No, I'm going to be your dad now, and as one Yorkshireman to another, I'm telling you you've got to come to London.' I continued to protest – it's too far, it'll take too long, I'm not finished at the demo yet, I'm still doing a signing – so Brian said, 'Mate, Lisa's asking where you are. She's invited us to a party in London, she's asked me to ask you, so you've got to come.'

My signature went from a clear 'James Martin' to a blur I was doing them so fast. I didn't stop to pose for photographs. It was chef's jacket off and into my supercharged

Elise. I drove like a bastard. I don't think I've ever driven so fast in my entire life, flat out all the way, straight into London. It wasn't long before I was parking up outside this club just over the road from Stringfellow's. I parked on a double yellow because I couldn't find a single yellow anywhere, then walked into the club cool as you like.

So we were in there, having a few beers, and a few more beers, and Brian asked how my car was. I told him I'd parked it on a double yellow so it had probably been towed, but what can you do, I've had a few beers anyway so I'll have to book a hotel for the night. The next minute I was in a cab heading towards Lisa's house. Just me and her. In a cab. We'd been chatting in the club and then I don't remember much other than her legs and her arse and suddenly being in this cab, not saying much but thinking, 'I'm in a cab with Lisa going back to her house. If this is my moment I'd better sober up very bloody rapidly.'

In the morning, first thing, I was straight out the front door, saying, 'See you later' and 'I'll give you a call' and all that – typical bloke – so quick that I didn't even stop to ask where the house was. I got outside, started off down the road and then realised that I had absolutely no idea where I was. I tried to find a taxi, but I was so far north I was practically on the M25 and there wasn't a black cab for miles. I turned my phone on and straight away Brian called, wanting to know all about the previous night. 'Mate,' I said to him, 'never mind last night, you've got to help me. I'm lost somewhere in North London.' Somehow Brian managed to find me on a map and he directed me to the nearest high street where I got a bus into central London and then a Tube over to the car pound on Park Lane to pay the £180 fine and pick up my Elise.

That was the last time I ever went on public transport, and with the mother of all hangovers it was a truly miserable experience.

Still, if that was a bad start to the day, it was nothing compared to what was to come. By lunchtime my agent Fiona was on the phone. She wanted to know what I'd been up to the night before. Now I hadn't told anyone anything, so I said, 'Nothing, I just went out for a couple of beers with Brian Turner.'

'Why have I had all the newspapers on the phone all morning then?' she came back.

I can always tell when Fiona's joking, and I knew straight away that she was being deadly serious.

'The *Sun* and the *Mirror* have got this story about you and an actress and they're going to run it as their front page.'

To be frank, I was now shitting myself at the thought of being a headline story. Fiona said that maybe I should think about saying something. Part of me was thinking, 'What's the point? If they're going to print the story, they're going to print it.' At the same time, though, I thought that not saying anything would look worse, like we'd done something wrong, which to the best of my memory we hadn't.

At about seven o'clock I finally decided to call the press, but from a phone box, because my dad had said once that if you phone from home they'll have your number. So I went to a phone box and phoned this guy up. I know now that these reporters never talk about the exact details of a story, they talk around it, keeping it as vague as possible, hoping that you'll fill in the gaps, but at the time I was new to this world and didn't know how any of it worked. I listened to what the journalist said, which wasn't much, just that they knew I'd spent the night with Lisa Faulkner. I told him it was all a load of bollocks, but he said that that was the story they were going to run, and the headline was going to be '11-Hour Sex Romp', to which my instant reaction was 'Nah, it was more like 15.' He said, 'Thanks very much, that's all I needed,' and put the phone down. And that was that.

In the end they held it until the Sunday. Sure enough, that morning I was woken at 6.30 by a phone call from my dad asking if I'd seen the paper. When I said I hadn't he told me that he had 20 copies if I wanted one and that he had to say he was surprised because 'I always thought you were queer'.

Two hours later I got a phone call from my mother.

'Have you got anything to say?' she asked.

I still hadn't been brave enough to go out and get a paper, so I said, 'No, not particularly.'

She wasn't impressed.

As it turned out, it wasn't so bad. They'd printed this amazing picture of Lisa from a photo shoot she'd just done, of her stepping into a Ferrari with these amazing heels and a split in her skirt that went all the way up to her arse, literally, so she looked fantastic; and then there was a picture of me in my bandanna under the headline 'Ready Steady Bonk: 15-Hour Sex Romp'. My mother didn't speak to me for about two months, but my dad thought it was hilarious.

To this day I don't know how the story got out. All I know is it didn't come from me, and there's no way on earth my fellow Yorkshireman Brian Turner would have grassed me up, even accidentally. It was my first taste of the tabloids, the moment when I realised just how powerful they could be. Unfortunately, it wouldn't be my last.

18 THE PERILS OF PUBLIC TRANSPORT

I absolutely hate public transport. It is, without exaggeration, my idea of hell. I once used it a lot, back when I lived and worked in London, and when I moved away and started making a bit more money I vowed I would never go back on it again, ever. And I've managed to stick to my word, apart from that one occasion when desperation, having my car impounded and being completely and utterly lost in North London forced me very much against my will to get on a bus and Tube train back from Lisa Faulkner's house.

I've never liked buses in particular. They're slow, you have to wait around for them for ages, and I just can't help associating them with old people. The irony of ironies is that my dad's actually driving a bus now. That's his part-time job. He drives a bus for the local park and ride. He said to me, 'Oh, you'll have to come on my bus one day,' and I went, 'No I bloody won't.' I don't do buses. When I worked in London I never really used to understand them anyway.

I never knew where any of them went and could never make head nor tail of the fiddly little timetables, so when I did use public transport it was usually the Tube. I could never afford black cabs, of course, and anyway, I never really got over that £22 charge to go from King's Cross to One Ninety Queen's Gate when I first arrived in London with just a £50 note in my pocket.

The Tube was all right, except for when I'd have to get the last train home after service, which would be full of pissed-up southerners coming home from a lairy Friday or Saturday night out. That was horrendous. Everything used to smell of wee and sick and spilt beer and chip fat and greasy fried chicken. It was just dreadful. Some nights, though, particularly when I was on the pastry section at One Ninety Queen's Gate, when we didn't finish until really late, sometimes three am, the last train was long gone and as you'd be starting work again at 7.30 we'd just clean down the bench and sleep on the marble slab. It was either that or sleep in the staff changing room. Either way, we were so tired we didn't care. We'd use our whites as a pillow, switch the lights off, and that was it, good night. It wasn't glamorous, but it was better than the other option: the night bus, so slow that by the time you got home it was time to come back again.

On the whole, though, I preferred to walk around London. There's plenty to see, and it's easier: you're not constantly going up and down escalators or being crammed in next to horrible sweaty people and being crushed by closing doors, and you don't have to climb over shopping trolleys and walking frames like you do on the buses.

I don't think my view of buses was helped at all by having once been knocked down by one. At one point when I lived in London I used to go everywhere on a push bike. Typically, it got nicked in the end, but before it did a bus knocked me off it when I was on my way to work one morning. It was at the junction where Kensington Church Street meets Kensington High Street. I was on the high street, coming from Olympia and heading towards the Albert Hall. I approached the junction, Kensington Church Street on my left, the lights were green, so I rode straight across and, BANG!, a bus came from the left straight into me. T-boned me and sent me flying. Apparently the driver had misread the lights at the end of Kensington Church Street. There was a green light and a red light, but the red light was for traffic filtering to the right, the green light was for traffic filtering to the left. He just saw it as a green light and accelerated across the junction just as I was coming the other way. I had my roll of knives in my ruck-sack and as I hit the floor they went absolutely everywhere. I just remember all these tourists standing around staring in horror, though I'm not sure what scared them most, seeing a cyclist being knocked off his bike by a big red London bus or the sight of 15 huge knives scattering all over the road. They must have thought I was a mass murderer or some kind of mad knifeman, a modern-day Jack the Ripper, only on a push bike. Luckily, no one lost any eyes or limbs as those sharp knives flew through the air. I just had a few cuts and bruises, and miraculously the bike was completely undamaged. It did nothing to improve my feelings towards public transport in general and buses in particular.

I think my biggest gripe with public transport is that it just doesn't work. Whenever I used it for work I was always late. If I drive I'm on time, if I go by public transport I'm late. It's as simple as that. It's ridiculously expensive too. I had a gig in Manchester one time and I had to be there by nine in the morning. Using public transport would have meant leaving my house at stupid o'clock in the morning and it would have cost the best part of £800 for me and my chef Chris, who works with me on all these big gigs, to get there with all our gear. We would have had to get the train from Winchester to London Waterloo, then a taxi (there was no way we were going on the Underground with all that gear) to Euston, then a train from there to Manchester Piccadilly. And then we'd have to come all the way back again. In total we would have been travelling for something like 15 hours, and the gig was only 30 minutes. It was a well-paid job so I thought, 'Sod it, we'll hire a plane.' Sixteen hundred quid it was, exactly double what it would have cost to go by public transport, and it was much quicker. We left my place at eight am and drove two miles up the road to Popham airfield where the plane was waiting for us. It took 45 minutes to fly there, I was at the venue bang on nine, I was on stage cooking at ten, I did a book signing and another demo, I cleared up, I left the venue and I was back home in my house by two o'clock that afternoon. On public transport, we worked out that we wouldn't have been back until gone midnight. All right, it cost double, but £1,600 isn't that much to charter a private plane, whereas £800 to get to Manchester on a train is scandalous. And I'd probably have been late.

It's only in this country that we struggle though. In France, Switzerland and Germany, public transport is bang on time. I went to Venice by train once. All right, it was the *Orient Express*, but it was incredible: there was a timetable, and every single station we hit on time, right the way across Europe. Why can't it be like that in this country? In reality, the only similarity is that to go from Winchester to Manchester on the train costs about as much as it does to go on the *Orient Express* across Europe.

Still, our roads aren't that much better. If you really want to get me started on a rant, bring up the congestion charge. Actually, please don't. It makes me so angry. It would be one thing if the money was actually spent on better roads, but it's not. Nowhere else in Europe has a road system in the mess ours is in. In France they don't have the same problems. Paris is the worst place on the planet to drive, but that's only because the Parisians are all crazy drivers. Otherwise it could teach London a thing or two. It's got more cars on the road but nowhere near as much traffic. How does that work? Don't get me wrong, I'm all for charging people to drive on motorways and everything else, just like they do in Germany and Switzerland, but then you've got to spend that money on building proper roads, like they have in Germany and Switzerland.

It's a truism that in life you really do get what you pay for – unless of course you're talking about British public transport.

19 A VERY ROYAL SCANDAL: THE LOTUS ELISE, PART II

To anyone who's ever owned one, the name Lotus has a special meaning: Lots Of Trouble, Usually Serious. My silver Elise was no exception. Admittedly they did warn me when I was having the engine supercharged that as well as upping the bhp the upgrade could have a negative effect on reliability, though to be fair, with 47,000 miles under its belt by now, the engine wasn't far off falling out of it anyway. When it ran, it ran brilliantly, but from day one there were always little niggles. The handbrake fell off, the roof fell off, the windscreen wipers fell off, and the spark plug leads fell off regularly, including once on the way to cater a function for Prince Charles at the Celtic Manor Hotel in Cardiff.

Thanks to Castle Howard's royal connections, I was no stranger to cooking for members of the royal family. I'd already cooked for the Queen Mother by the age of twelve, and when I was working for Antony Worrall Thompson at One Ninety Queen's Gate both Princess Diana and the

Prince of Wales regularly ate in the downstairs restaurant. So while I avoid politics like the plague and refuse to do anything at 10 Downing Street because I don't want to be seen to be endorsing anyone's agenda, I'm always happy to cook for the royal family, especially the Prince of Wales, who's a big promoter of British produce, a subject close to my heart. The gig at the Celtic Manor Hotel was a big press event to celebrate Welsh beef and Welsh lamb, and as Prince Charles was attending they wanted a well-known chef. I was doing *Ready Steady Cook* that day, but Fiona got me the early show so I could be out of there by 1.15 pm, which would give me just about enough time to get to Cardiff by four, when Prince Charles was due to arrive.

One fifteen on the dot I was in the Elise with all my stuff. My knives and my spotless white chef's jacket (which I'd got wardrobe staff at *Ready Steady Cook* to iron for me) were on the passenger seat and I was off to Cardiff. I was hoofing it because I didn't have long to get there, and I was just going past Reading services when the car started coughing, clucking and spluttering. 'That's got to be one of the bloody spark plug leads again,' I thought, so I pulled over on to the hard shoulder. The engine in the Elise is in the rear, just behind the tiny boot – literally only big enough for your wallet – which you have to lean over to get to the engine bay. On mine, though, there wasn't anything to keep the flappy plastic lid open while you were in there, so there I was, at the side of the road, hazard lights flashing, farting about trying to reattach this spark plug lead under a boot lid propped open with one of my knives.

I was still 100 miles from Cardiff, it was two o'clock, my hands were now covered in oil and I was just starting to panic when I heard a police siren. 'This is all I need,' I thought, but when I looked round it wasn't a police car pulling up behind me to find out what I was doing, it was Prince Charles's motorcade – two motorbike outriders, a police car, two Range Rovers, a Cavalier and another motorbike, all lights blazing – steaming along the fast lane on their way to Cardiff. To meet me!

After a few more minutes of frantic fiddling I managed to get the spark plug lead back on. I wiped my greasy hands as best I could on my jeans, jumped in the car, fired it up and blatted it as hard as I dared. I caught the motorcade about 10 miles from Cardiff and undertook them in the middle lane.

As I was getting out of the car at the hotel, Prince Charles's motorcade was pulling into the car park. My hands were still grimy, my jeans were covered in grease, and so too was my beautifully ironed, immaculately white chef's jacket, once I'd grabbed it from the passenger seat. I ran like a nutcase into reception, which was full of people who had obviously been expecting me a lot earlier because they looked as panicked as I probably did. They directed me straight to the kitchen, and I ran through, pulling on my chef's jacket with its greasy finger marks.

I'd been in the hotel no more than 30 seconds when I walked out through the kitchen doors and into a room full of staff and press, making it to my spot just as Prince Charles entered the dining room. In front of me was a huge silver platter with a huge piece of beef on it. To my left there must have been a hundred photographers, cameramen and press. On my right there was a long line of dignitaries I hadn't yet met. Prince Charles was making his way down, one by one, shaking hands and saying hello. At last he got to me.

'Hello, James, how are you?' he said.

'Very well, thank you, very well,' I replied, trying to hide my dirty hands.

With that, he looked at this great piece of beef on the platter in front of us and said, 'May I?'

Now, I'd never clapped eyes on this piece of beef before, but I couldn't very well say no to the heir to the throne. But as I was carving a slice from this big, beautifully roasted four-rib rack of beef I knew something wasn't quite right, though I couldn't for the life of me work out what. Then, just as he was putting the meat in his mouth, it hit me: the beef was still on the bone. This was at the height of the mad cow disease scare. You weren't allowed to serve beef on the bone. It was totally illegal. BSE was the biggest news story there was. British beef exports were being banned left, right and centre, and every day the newspapers were running huge headlines warning of the dangers of serving beef on the bone. And I'd just given the Prince of Wales a big slice of it in front of a room full of journalists.

Unfortunately, just as I clocked it, so did one of the journalists, and the news went straight down the row of photographers like wildfire. The second Prince Charles put the beef in his mouth everything suddenly went into a slow-motion blur as the whole room exploded in a blaze of flashes. For the whole of the time he spent chewing this slice of beef, possibly the longest minute or so of my life, it was absolute mayhem. The Prince himself seemed totally oblivious to the whole thing. I vaguely remember him saying that it was lovely and thanking me, but I was in a state of shock, trying to work out what had just happened and bemoaning the fact that it would probably end up being my fault even though I'd only been in the building for a few minutes.

As Prince Charles walked out of the room, a press woman turned to me and asked what all that had been about. I told her that the beef was on the bone, but before she'd had a chance even to try to deal with that information all hell broke loose. Minutes later I was running out of the hotel, followed by the world's media. Sky were going out live, the BBC were turning up with satellite dishes, and I was running for the Lotus. I booted it back home to Winchester in record time. I made it back just in time to see myself as the top story on the evening news.

Ten minutes later my mobile rang. It was my mother. 'So, been in Cardiff then? Have you got anything to say?'

Next day it was on the front page of all the papers: 'Prince Charles Defies Ban', 'Prince Eats Beef On Bone', 'Celebrity Chef Serves Prince Banned Beef'. The truth was, he didn't notice it was on the bone and neither did I, until it was too late. I'd been so late for the event that I'd had nothing to do with the cooking. Even so, I thought that would pretty much be the end of my dealings with the royal family. Having inadvertently dragged him into a political scandal, I certainly didn't think I'd ever be asked to cook for Prince Charles again.

Clearly he's not one to hold grudges. A few years later he personally invited me to cook a meal at Clarence House, again to promote British beef, but this time for a room full of the greatest chefs ever to come out of France, including Michel Troisgros and Alain Ducasse, both three-star Michelin chefs, so he obviously still had faith in me. He was also very gracious. In the hour and a half he spent in the kitchen with me he didn't once mention that meeting in Cardiff, the beef on the bone or the media fallout.

Sadly, my relationship with my supercharged yet unreliable Elise wasn't so long-lasting. After those 47,000 very eventful miles together I think we'd had enough of each other and it was time to go our separate ways before I got into any more trouble, or the engine fell out. Three months after that spark plug lead popped out on the way to Cardiff the Elise was gone.

20 *THE AUDI CONVERT*

The car that rekindled my love for all things Audi and undid the emotional scarring caused by my father's early misguided attempts at Vorsprung Durch Technik was the S4.

Back in the eighties, when I was growing up, if you couldn't quite afford a Lamborghini Countach (white) or a Ferrari Testarossa (red), there was only one car to have, the Audi Quattro. The first car to feature both Audi's new four-wheel drive and a turbocharger, with its wide wheel arches, big alloys and digital dashboard it was easily the most exciting thing on four wheels – especially if you were sitting at home glued to the TV watching the legend that was female French rally driver Michèle Mouton blasting through the woods and flying over dirt-track peaks somewhere in Italy in the World Rally Championship. White or red, it really didn't get any better than the Audi Quattro. Except for maybe the Audi Sport Quattro, which had even wider wheel arches and bigger alloys to go with its more powerful 303bhp engine. Oh to have had one of those!

Instead, as you know, when my father finally decided to get with the cool dads and give his passion for dreadful French cars a rest, he inexplicably went out and bought that gold Audi 80 and that lime green Audi 100 with a lime green cloth interior – migraine-inducing stuff. If the visual horror of those two cars wasn't enough to put me off Audis for life, then the humiliation of all my mates seeing me getting out of a day-glo snot-coloured car almost was. Put it this way, it was a long time before I could pass an Audi dealership without shuddering.

At the time, work was going really well, I was earning good money, and despite my youth I felt the need for something a bit more stylish, sophisticated and, after the Lotus Elise, reliable. To be honest, I only went to look at the S4 Coupé because my mum's fella, Pete, said it was good, and what Pete didn't know about cars, especially Audis, wasn't worth knowing. In fact, take Pete to an Audi showroom and nine times out of ten he'll know more about all the different models, their specs and options than the salesmen. As I said, Pete's a proper car nut, like me, and despite being on his fourth TT he's a pretty good judge of cars. So I took him and Mum to Audi York to have a look at one. I looked it over, liked it, took it for a test drive, got back to the showroom, said, 'I'll take it,' and wrote a cheque for the full amount there and then. I'll never forget my mum's face. A look of shock and horror. She just kept saying, 'Can you afford it?' and 'Are you sure it's not too expensive?' I think that was the moment when my mum truly realised that things had changed for her son. And it wasn't just the money. I think the episode had a greater significance for her because, despite my father's earlier purchases, my mum really loves Audis and she knew and understood what I was buying. The significance of writing that cheque was different for me: just 18 months earlier I'd been over £30,000 in debt. That's the power of television for you.

The transaction wasn't quite that easy though. I wrote the cheque and handed it over to the salesman who went off to the back office, only to return a couple of minutes later to say that he was very sorry and all that but they couldn't accept it. It was because it was a Coutts cheque, and they didn't accept them. My mum then turned her look of horror on to the salesman and spent the next few minutes trying to explain to him what Coutts was and that everyone accepted their cheques. Meanwhile, I was on the phone to my personal banker Richard explaining the situation. 'Let me speak to him,' he said, and five minutes later everyone was all smiles and I was being handed the keys to my new S4.

It was a great car. It instantly converted me and, the Nicky Clarke cut 'n' blowdry overtones of the TT aside, I've been a big Audi fan ever since. A couple of years ago, on the recommendation of both Pete and my mate and fellow car fanatic Jay Kay, I bought the sports estate, the RS4 Avant, which at the time of writing is without a doubt the best car I own. That said, I test-drove the R8, Audi's £90,000 Le Mans-inspired supercar, for my motoring column in the *Mail on Sunday* when it first came out. From the sound of the high-revving V8 to the way it goes round corners (hard and fast) it's a serious car, one of the best I've ever driven. I want one. So who knows, by the time you read this, if I can swing it and I can find a way round the two-year waiting list, I might have a new favourite Audi sitting in the garage.

21 *A CONSIDERED BUY: THE FERRARI 360, PART I*

All my life I've only ever had one real problem with cars: I've never really been able to afford them. Whatever I've wanted has always been just that bit more than I can comfortably manage. It's always been the same, and it probably always will be.

Whatever anyone sitting at home watching TV (or reading this book) might think, you certainly don't set out to become a chef in order to be a millionaire. Working six days a week for six months without so much as a day off or a thank you, and all for crap money, I can honestly say it's one job you just do for the love of it. Whatever grand ambitions I might have had all those years ago when I announced to my family at the kitchen table that I was going to be a head chef at 30, have my own restaurant at 35 and a Ferrari by the age of 40, I never really imagined that being a chef would bring me anything other than the roof over my head. On plenty of occasions it didn't even do that.

All of which for several years was frustrating, because as

far back as I can remember I've wanted a Ferrari. It began as a childhood dream while parking cars at Castle Howard; it intensified as I watched Tom Selleck tearing around Hawaii in his little red 308GTS; and then it became the obsession of a penniless pastry chef who stared through London showroom windows at night. Owning a Ferrari has always been the ultimate for me. Ferraris aren't like other cars. Anyone who's ever seen, heard, touched or sat in one will tell you that they're unique. There's a passion and excitement to them you just don't get with any other machine. It's like Ferrari leather has been genetically engineered to smell like money. It's the same with Sunseeker yachts: they smell of £50 notes. While fivers smell of sweat and hard work, fifties smell of Givenchy.

Not that I ever really thought of a Ferrari as a status symbol. They are, but that's not why I wanted one. Of course, for someone like me to own one would be a massive achievement. For a small boy from Yorkshire who was always thought of as a bit thick at school, who was packed off to London with nothing but a £50 note and a train ticket and who returned with a wealth of experience but a mountain of debt, for him to own a Ferrari just like the ones that used to park at Castle Howard, Chewton Glen and the Hotel Du Vin would be amazing. Lad made good and all that. But I wanted one long before I even knew what a status symbol was. I don't remember ever being able to think of anything more exciting than a Ferrari.

Unfortunately, as I said, most chefs are considered to be doing all right if they've got four walls, a ceiling and a bed to call their own. Still, it was clear to anyone who came to my flat in Winchester that as I approached the age of 25 I was doing a bit better than all right. It looked nothing from the side of the road, but inside it was massive. It had this big staircase, and because I had grown up around Castle Howard with all its great old furniture, I'd kitted it out with loads of antiques. I'd go to auctions and antique markets and buy really old Italian chests and big ornate gilt mirrors, so the place looked like a miniature Castle Howard, tassels and bloody great sofas everywhere.

I'd been doing *Ready Steady Cook* for a while by then, and what with the TV work, demonstrations, appearances, food festivals and catering gigs coming in off the back of it, for the first time in my life I was doing pretty well for myself. More importantly, for once in my life I was being sensible. I'd finally paid off all my debts, making it practically the first time I'd been debt-free since leaving school. I'd bought and paid for my flat, I'd decorated it, I'd even bought a decent bed. Actually I was too busy working to go and buy a bed so I'd given my mum my credit card and asked her to go and buy me one. She went to Harrods and spent shed-loads on one, with linen. I couldn't believe it. I just wanted a bed, any old bed would have done, but she insisted that a good bed is one of the most important things you'll ever own because you're in it for a long time, and she was right. I've still got that bed and it is amazing. The only problem is, I never want to get out of it!

With the bed delivered, my antiques arranged and my flat resembling a stately home, the only thing missing was a decent kitchen. Again, it was a question of time not money. I wanted to be sure of what my dream kitchen would look like. This is how sensible and grown up I'd become. For once I was getting my priorities 'right'. I even had a practical car, an Audi S4 saloon, the perfect vehicle for a busy chef with loads of pots and pans and ingredients to carry from one end of the country to the other.

The thing with me, though, is that I've never really been able to do the 'right' thing – not for very long anyway. It's not that I want to be different just for the sake of it. I'm not one of these people who goes left because everyone else is going right. I just question things, like the logic that says something has to be done in a certain way. And when opportunities come up, I tend to dive in and make the most of them, not talk myself out of it like most other people would. So it's at times like these, when everything's set fair and going along nicely, that fate has a habit of stepping in and making my life a little bit more interesting.

So, sure enough, one day I was at the House and Garden Show, I'd just finished a demonstration, and a woman from the crowd came up to me and asked if I had a kitchen in my house. I had no idea why she'd want to know, but I told her that as it happened, no, I didn't; all I had was the shit tip that was there when I moved in, a really horrible thing with an electric stove. She then offered to design me a kitchen and install it in my flat, for next to nothing. Some things are just too good to refuse, so I went and had a look at what her company, Underwood, were doing and was so impressed with the amazing bespoke kitchens they made, proper top-of-the-range stuff, that not only did I take her up on her very kind offer, I later invested in the company.

Now, the crucial point here isn't that I was about to become the proud owner of an absolutely stunning bespoke kitchen, or that this chance meeting turned into a great business opportunity. No. The crucial point here is that getting this great deal on the kitchen meant that every penny of the £50 grand sitting in my bank account, a large chunk of which had been earmarked for the design and installation of a top-of-the-range bespoke kitchen, was now suddenly just, well, doing nothing.

Most 'right'-thinking people with £50 grand would probably go in search of a nice healthy interest rate. Me, I was straight down the newsagent's for a copy of *Top Marques* magazine. I had a quick flick through the classifieds section and there it was, as fateful as having a complete stranger offer you a free kitchen: Ferrari 355, Red, £51,000. Perfect. That would leave me with a few hundred quid as my life savings, which was good, because it meant I wasn't being totally reckless.

I jumped into my sensible and practical Audi S4 and drove down to the dealership, which was in Petworth in Sussex, near where my father had been stationed when he was a copper. I went by myself and didn't tell anyone I was going. When I pulled up in front of the showroom I could see it through the window, just sitting there in the middle of the floor, a shiny bright red Ferrari 355. Beautiful. Absolutely beautiful.

I walked in. I was wearing jeans and a T-shirt and

because I'd just pulled up in the Audi S4 no one paid me any attention. I went straight over to the car and gave it a good look over, thinking, 'This is all right, this.' It had the F1 paddle gear shift on the steering column, it wasn't the manual with the stick that no one wanted, it was right-hand drive, it had a cream leather interior ... quite frankly, it was the bollocks.

Still no one was paying me any attention, so I got in. Sure enough, the salesman came over. 'Would you like to know anything about the car, sir?' he asked, then he began giving me its life story: one careful owner, 4,000 miles, F1 gear shift, which everyone wants ... This was only the second time I'd ever sat in a Ferrari, after the 308 back at Castle Howard, and it felt exactly the same. It smelt exactly the same. It had *that* smell, the smell all Ferraris have. I was sold. I wanted it.

Obviously it was either a very slow day or the salesman noticed that my eyes were out on stalks and I was practically reaching for my wallet, because the next thing I knew he was asking if I'd like to go for a spin. He put the trade plates on and we were off. He was driving, which was probably just as well because all I could think as we drove along was that this was absolutely bloody unbelievable.

We returned to the showroom, and I knew I was having it. But being a Yorkshireman, and having grown up with my father who never liked to pay the full price for anything, I asked the salesman if he'd be willing to do a deal on it. Part of me just wanted to give him the money, grab the keys and go; another part was desperately trying to play it cool, telling the salesman he needed to come down a bit. To my amazement, he actually thought about it.

I was playing it cool, he was thinking about the best price he could do, and then, over his shoulder, over the other side of the showroom, I saw these guys wheeling in another car, an absolutely stunning black on black Ferrari 360.

The 360 was the replacement for the 355. It had literally only just been launched in the UK, but this one was a left-hand drive import, just a few months old. Hard top. F1 paddle shift. Black paint, black leather. Four thousand miles on the clock. Full service history. I mean, the 355 was fantastic, but this was something else – £80 grand's worth of something else. I thought, 'Bloody hell, here we go.' I knew what was coming next.

If I part-exchanged the Audi, I reckoned I could get almost £20 grand for it. Plus the £55 grand I had in the bank, that gave me £70 grand or thereabouts. If I financed the rest … The salesman was trying to lean me more towards the 355 because he knew I couldn't really afford the 360. After giving it a good look over, I decided that the sensible thing to do (relatively speaking) was to go off and have a think about it, so I drove about an hour down the road to a nice little pub and had something to eat. All I could think about was the black 360. Truth be told, the 355, great though it was, wasn't even in the picture any more.

I decided I'd go back and have a sit in the 360, see how it felt. Of course it felt amazing, and within about 15 minutes the deal was done: they agreed to give me £19,000 for the Audi and I financed the rest. I went in with £55,000 max and a dream of buying a red 355, I came out the owner of a stunning black 360 and eight grand in debt.

Part of the deal was that I couldn't drive the Audi any more than 250 miles between that moment and when I went back to collect the 360. So I drove back to Winchester and then didn't drive the S4 again. I just stayed in for the next week, waiting patiently for the funds to clear and the paperwork to go through. I didn't tell anybody what I'd done, not my mum, my dad, my sister or my friends. I just carried on, as best I could, as normal.

The only person who knew anything about the car was a guy called Mark Papworth, who owned garages in Winchester where rich people stored their cars. My flat had no garage, and in a matter of days I was going to have an £80 grand Ferrari and nowhere to park it, so I went to see Mark to see if he'd rent me a space. I told him what the car was and he said, 'Yep, that's fine.' It was a tenner a week, which I thought sounded all right. I gave him my details, and he asked, 'Who's your insurance company?' I told him I hadn't got that far yet and he did a double-take, laughed, and suddenly looked very worried. He told me to prepare myself for a shock: a 24-year-old man who'd never had anything remotely like a Ferrari 360 before … it would add up to a pretty hefty premium. And he was right. After phoning around for a while the best quote I could get was £2,800 for the year, third party. I didn't have £2,800 so I put it on my credit card thinking that if I'd done the maths right and I didn't eat I could probably just about pay it off at the end of the month.

A week went by, still no one knew about the car, and at last I got the call I'd been waiting for, telling me I could pick up my 360 the following day. I'd invited my dad down from Yorkshire to come and have a look at the new flat and stay over. He looked round the place, which barring the kitchen was pretty much finished, and said, 'Bloody hell, lad, you've done all right here.' We had a bite to eat and a nice evening together, then the next morning I asked if he'd like to go for a drive, maybe head down towards Petworth where he used to be stationed.

In the car he was telling me all these stories about where he'd worked and the things he'd got up to, tales of chasing armed robbers in his old MkII Jag and single-handedly disarming a deranged squaddie who was smashing up a pub – all the old war stories. We drove past this pub he used to go to and he asked if we could pop in and see if the same landlord was still running the place. We went in and sure enough it was the same bloke behind the bar. He and my dad got talking like they were best buddies, and all the time I was thinking, 'I've got to be at the Ferrari dealership by 12.30 to pick up the new car, the one my dad knows nothing about.' As far as he was concerned we were just out for a drive. Trying not to be too obvious, and without giving the game away, I managed to break up the reunion and get him back into the car.

When we got to the showroom I casually drove past, slowing down to look in the window. I said something about popping in to have a look at the cars, as we were there. We doubled back, pulled up outside, and straight away he said, 'Well, there you go, son, there's your dream.' He was pointing to the red 355 sitting in the middle of the showroom. Next to it was the black 360, my black 360. Still looking at it, he shook his head and added, 'You know, one day ... well, you never know.'

As we walked in through the showroom door he suddenly went straight into Dad mode. He straightened his tie and started acting all serious, being the main man, walking around touching everything, nodding his approval, running his hand along the bodywork of the 355, looking through the window of the 360. We were looking at the cars for about ten minutes while the salesman I'd been dealing with finished up with another customer. By the time he came over to ask if I had my documents we were both sat in the 360 playing with the switches, admiring the stitching, taking in big lungfuls of the leather.

I went off to the office to sign the forms and get the keys, leaving my dad in the car thinking that I was completing paperwork so that I could take it for a test drive. When I returned he was still sitting there, as transfixed as I had been a week earlier. I asked him if he was ready to take it out for a bit of a spin. Still none the wiser, he fastened his seat belt. I fired it up, and just as we were pulling out of the showroom I turned to him and said, 'Dad, you know when I was seven years old and I said I wanted a Ferrari by the time I was 40? Well, I've done it. This is it.'

My dad looked at me, and he knew from my face that I was deadly serious. There was no mucking about on his part, no 'yeah right, course you have' like most dads would have done. He just looked at me and, without saying a word, burst into tears.

That day, sat there on the forecourt of that Ferrari dealership, was the one and only time I've ever seen my father cry. As I pulled off down the road he looked at me through his tears and just said, 'I can't believe you've done it.' Which of course set me off. We drove off up the road, both of us balling our eyes out, father and son, tears streaming down our faces.

Then I looked down at the dashboard and as my eyes welled up again I noticed that the fuel gauge was saying the tank had only about a fiver's worth of petrol in it. I was barrelling down the road in my dream Ferrari, third party insurance, tears streaming down my face, my father crying like a baby, my bank account empty, my credit card maxed, and to top it all I was about to run out of petrol. Next petrol station we saw I pulled in, with no idea how I was going to pay. Before I'd even opened the driver's door, how-ever, my dad got out, turned to me and said, 'This one's on me, son.'

He's a man of very few words, my father, not given to outward displays of emotion, but as he stood there filling my Ferrari up, watching the numbers flicking past on the pump with a look of 'How much?' on his face, I knew he was proud of me.

A hundred quid and a full tank later, we went for a proper spin, back to the pub we'd stopped at earlier, where he treated me to a late lunch. He told me to order whatever I wanted and we had smoked salmon and the best fillet steak I've ever eaten. I ate like a pig and had one of the happiest meals of my life.

In the car back he didn't say much. In fact, I don't remember him saying anything at all. He just sat there, not exactly smiling, but you could tell. He didn't really want to show it, but inside he was beaming.

22 MY OTHER CAR'S A FERRARI: THE VAUXHALL CORSA

Forget the cookbooks, TV and foxtrotting in the semi-final of *Strictly Come Dancing* – I swear my mother's proudest moment was when Vauxhall turned me into a cardboard cut-out and stuck me in the window of their showrooms. Don't ask me why, but she loved it. She told all her friends and they all went out and got these lifesize free-standing pictures of me in my bandanna and chef's whites, which had a little Vauxhall logo on them. My mum kept hers in the living room, just so she didn't forget what I looked like.

I've never been entirely sure how the gig came about or why they wanted me. I suppose they were looking for someone who was young, on TV and known for liking their cars. Apart from being turned into cardboard, all I had to do was turn up at the odd press event, do a couple of book signings and make an appearance at the London Motor Show, which I would probably have gone to anyway. In return I got a free, top-of-the-range blue Corsa 1.6 GTi for a year and a stunning Wonderbra model girlfriend.

I was still storing my 360 in Mark Papworth's garages, so the Corsa came in pretty handy for driving between there and home and other everyday back-and-forth journeying. There was a price to pay though. To get to Mark's I had to drive down the high street, and every time I went past the pub, without fail, I got bombarded with jeers and abuse from the lads standing outside having a pint who were used to seeing (and hearing) me blatting it up the road in my Ferrari. 'All right, James, got a new motor?' was a favourite. 'Work not so good? Tosser!' If there was anyone who needed one of those 'My other car's a Ferrari' stickers on the back window, it was me.

The real pay-off from the Vauxhall deal came at the motor show. There was no specific role for me other than just to be there, and I only had to make a brief appearance at that. So on the first day I drove up there in the Corsa with a stack of books (which then would have been *Delicious: The Deli Cookbook*), set myself up on the stand and just hung about. All of a sudden the stand exploded into life – lights, music, dry ice, and literally from out of nowhere all these dancers appeared and began to cavort around the new Corsa to this banging Euro-dance track, 'Communication (Somebody Answer the Phone)'. In the centre of the stage is this stunning 6-foot model type who's dancing around in a figure-hugging dress, the kind that's kept decent with nipple tape, singing the chorus line.

Almost as quickly as it had started, it was over, back to the star attraction (me), the car and a pile of books. Five minutes later, the model is standing next to me asking what

I'm doing there. I said I was just hanging about, signing a few books. She pointed to the chef's whites and said, 'So you're not working then?'

'No, no,' I replied. 'Apparently I just have to make an appearance.'

'Oh, so you can take me for a drink then.'

We went for a drink and had something to eat. Her name was Sinta Soekadarova. She was half Indonesian, half Czech, and when she wasn't singing 'Somebody Answer the Phone' she was a Wonderbra model, and when she wasn't modelling Wonderbras she was a Bond girl. (In *The World Is Not Enough*, Pierce Brosnan wanders into a bar, puts on a pair of X-ray glasses, looks at these two girls at the bar and sees they've got guns tucked into their underwear. The girl with the dark hair is Sinta.) After I met her, my interest in seeing the rest of the motor show and looking at all the cars suddenly went straight out of the window. To be honest, I couldn't even concentrate on eating my chicken sandwich when we went on to have lunch; I was too busy looking at her dress trying to work out if it was really stuck on with Sellotape.

There, on the Vauxhall stand at the London Motor Show, next to the new Corsa 1.6 GTi and a cardboard cut-out of yours truly, began a beautiful relationship. Sinta and I were together for two years in the end.

She was a bit mad, but great fun. It was all going along quite happily until the curse of *Hello!* magazine struck. I'd never done *Hello!* or *OK* before, and I'd never do either of them again. Once was enough. They call it 'the curse of

Hello!' because invariably whatever happy couple is featured, seen casually draped over scatter cushions on the bed or leaning against the mantelpiece lovingly staring into each other's eyes are usually divorced or separated by the time the magazine hits the shelves, no matter how long they've been together or how happy they were before the *Hello!* stylists came along and rearranged their wardrobe and their home. We were no different. Three weeks after the shoot it was all over.

My mum's still got that cut-out though.

23 IT'S ONLY METAL: THE FERRARI 360, PART II

Antony Worrall Thompson has always been there at the pivotal moments in my life. My first job out of catering college was in his restaurant; my first big break on TV was on *Ready Steady Cook*, a show on which he was a regular; my agent Fiona, who completely turned my career around, was Antony's recommendation; I even inherited *Saturday Kitchen* from him. So maybe, in some perverse and twisted way, it was fitting that he was there, lurking in the background, when the bottom literally dropped out of my world – or at least out of the back of my Ferrari.

I'd had my black 360 about a year when it happened. That car was my pride and joy, and as clichéd as that sounds, it was true. I took exceptional care of it. I used the Corsa for day-to-day driving because I didn't want to put the miles on the Ferrari. On rare occasions I even took the train – that's how careful I was being with that car. If I was driving it, it was a pretty special occasion, and one such time was Antony's 50th birthday party in Oxford, for which I was doing the catering.

Thankfully, the 360 was designed with golfers in mind. It'll never win awards for boot space, but I could just about get all my gear in there, leaving the passenger seat free for Sinta and the cake. Antony's partner Jay had asked me to make an Antony-shaped cake and I'd spent ages on a little Worrall Thompson made out of marzipan and icing. It sat in the passenger footwell all the way up there.

Antony's party was great – he loved the cake and everybody had a good time. The following morning we left really early because I had an appointment to view a flat in Southampton. This place had just come on the market and I'd been told that there was likely to be a lot of interest in it so I was keen to get in there early. We were driving along the A34, heading back to Winchester so that I could drop all my stuff off and get changed, when suddenly there was an almighty BANG! out the rear end. I wasn't speeding, I wasn't banging the revs, I was doing a comfortable 70 miles an hour, because I like to cruise – and a car as cool as the 360 was made for cruising, especially if you've got a Wonderbra model sitting next to you.

Another BANG!

I looked in my rear-view mirror and saw to my horror that the glass engine cover, which is roughly where the rear windscreen would be on most cars, had gone. The car was losing speed and power, slowing down, slowing down, and the next time I looked in the rear-view mirror it was as if someone had emptied out a wheelbarrow of Ferrari engine parts all over the motorway. It was about eight am on a Sunday, so luckily there wasn't much traffic, which was just as well because along with the bits and pieces was a massive oil slick.

I pulled over, put my hazard lights on and inspected the damage. It didn't take a Ferrari-qualified mechanic to tell me that the cam belt had come off and shot one of the pistons through the glass engine cover, and the rest of the engine had gone with it. For a couple of minutes I just stood there, staring in disbelief at the A34, which now had parts of my dream car scattered all over it. The only person I could think to call was Mark Papworth. After a few 'you're jokings' and a bit of swearing, he told me to sit tight and he'd come and pick me and the car up with his trailer. In the meantime I phoned Pippa, my PA, to tell her I might be a bit late for the viewing. I was only about 10 miles outside Winchester, which was where Pippa also lived, so she suggested she come and pick me up, and if we hoofed it we might just make it to the flat in time. Because he was storing the 360 Mark already had a spare set of keys, so I called him back, told him I was going to go to Southampton with Pippa, and if he could still pick the car up I'd meet him back at the garages later.

When Pippa arrived, Sinta and I jumped in her car and I left my pride and joy (or what was left of it) all alone on the hard shoulder with nothing but a pile of twisted engine parts and scrap metal for company. Thankfully, Mark didn't hang about. As he told it, when he arrived to retrieve the 360 someone was already preparing to hoist it on to a trailer. Had he arrived a couple of minutes later there might not have been anything left for him to collect.

Next day, he delivered the car to the Ferrari dealership in the New Forest. Luckily, the cam belt had let go one week before the end of the warranty. Obviously, it wasn't an ideal situation having the back drop out of the car I'd dreamed of owning since I was a child, but at least it wouldn't cost me anything to have it repaired.

Ferrari didn't quite see it like that. They came back saying that it wasn't covered by the warranty as it counted as 'wear and tear'. Wear and tear? I'd treated the car with kid gloves. I'd driven through Winchester in a Vauxhall Corsa and been mercilessly mocked by the locals in order to spare that engine. I'd even got on a train to avoid 'wear and tear'. Ferrari said they wanted twenty-five grand to put it right. After a few heated debates and a lot of talk about lawyers, Ferrari relented and agreed to return my 360 to its former glory free of charge.

It was a close-run thing though, and times like that make you realise just how easily things can be taken away from you. My mother tried to make me feel better by pointing out, just as Ferrari were telling me they wouldn't touch it for less than £25,000, 'It's only metal.' In response, I said that it may indeed only be metal, but it was metal I hadn't yet finished paying for. All my money was in that car, and if Ferrari hadn't done the decent thing I'd have been in a deep financial hole – in fact far deeper than I knew at the time.

24 *A KICK IN THE NUTS: THE FERRARI 360, PART III*

In one way or another I've always tied all my money up in cars. They're the first things I think of buying when I get paid. If you examined my monthly outgoings, the vast majority would relate to cars; if you looked at the paperwork for almost every bank loan or credit application I've ever taken out or made, chances are there would be a make and model number on there somewhere. I've never had savings long term, and on the rare occasions I've had surplus money in the bank, it was only there because I hadn't quite decided which motor to buy with it. Meaning that, apart from the four walls around me and the roof over my head, cars are my biggest asset.

Sometimes that's been a good thing. I never buy cars as an investment, but there have been times when I've put all my money, and more, into one, sold it a couple of weeks, months or years later and made enough to put down a substantial deposit on a house, or to build more garages to fill with more cars. On the downside, never keeping anything back for a rainy day means that when there's a torrential downpour, usually courtesy of the taxman, there's only one thing for it. Throughout my professional life a tax bill has usually been swiftly followed by an ad in the back of *Top Marques* magazine.

On the very rare occasions I have put money into something without an engine, the best returns have always come from something food-related. Investing in Underwood Kitchens, the company that approached me at the House and Garden Show and asked if I wanted a new kitchen, has quite literally paid dividends. My deli in Winchester, which I bought with the help of my old mate Alex Edwards, who along with Harvey Jones used to take me to the pub and pay for all my drinks when I was at the Hotel Du Vin and didn't have a pot to piss in, was a runaway success from the second we opened the door. The one time I tried to make cars my business rather than my pleasure, though, I got my arse well and truly burned.

My TV career had taken off big style, I had my two-bedroom mini Castle Howard in Winchester, I had a gorgeous girlfriend and I was driving my dream Ferrari. Maybe I was being a bit naive, but it seemed like everything I touched was turning to gold. So when someone suggested investing in a chauffeur business, I jumped at it. At the time, Robert Kilroy-Silk owned a fleet of cars and had a chauffeuring business as a sideline to his TV work, and he was doing all right out of it. What with my love of cars, it sounded like a great idea. I'd put together a business plan and was looking at brand-new Chryslers to start off the fleet. But it didn't work out and I ended up losing all the money I'd put into it.

It was practically every penny I had. I was back to square one again. I didn't know where to turn. I didn't want to tell my dad because I knew he would just tell me I'd been an idiot, and I could work that out for myself. I didn't want to tell my mum because she would have freaked out, which I was already doing anyway. Things had gone from being unbelievably good to being about as bad as they could be.

And then it got worse.

A couple of weeks later I got my first big tax bill. I was expecting it to be big because my accountant had told me it was going to be. Then I got a phone call from him. He said he was sorry, he must have made a mistake some-where along the line, because instead of being £40 grand it was actually £96 grand. At that stage I had £15,000 in my account and about six weeks to find the rest. On top of that a production company that owed me £22,000 went bust, and another company for whom I'd done a string of cooking demos, events and appearances was refusing to pay up £28,000. I couldn't do much about the company that had gone bust, but there was no way I was going to just forget about £28,000. I couldn't afford to. There was nothing else for it: if the guy who ran the company wasn't going to hand it over, I'd just have to go and get it.

Fiona, my agent, gave me the guy's address. I rounded up some mates and we jumped into my Vauxhall Corsa and drove to this address in Maidenhead. When we got there I phoned Fiona to double-check the details she'd given me because instead of an office we were outside a big house on a private housing estate with a driveway full of cars – a new Cosworth, a TVR and a Lotus Elise. Fiona said it was the only address she had so I rang the buzzer.

'Hi, it's James Martin, I'm here for my cheque.'

The person who answered denied all knowledge and said that I'd got the wrong address. Thinking that it might just be possible we'd got the wrong house we drove around the estate, until it clicked that it was definitely the right house and my money was actually sitting out on the driveway. We went back and tried again.

'No, no one lives here by that name,' said the guy on the intercom.

I told him I didn't believe him and that he might want to come and give me my cheque before his cars ended up on the receiving end of our anger. We saw this guy look out of the window at my mate, cricket bat in hand, taking aim at the windscreen of the Elise. He came belting out of the house with his cheque book in hand, shaking like a leaf. I told him the cheque had better not bounce because if it did we'd be back.

Luckily the cheque cleared, and along with the £15,000 in my account I now had £43,000 for the Inland Revenue. Of course that still left me £53,000 short. There was nothing for it. I phoned Mark Papworth and told him I wanted to sell the Ferrari.

'What?' he said. 'The 360? But you love that car. Why would you want to do that?'

I didn't have the balls to tell him the truth. Instead, I told him that after the engine dropped out of it I wasn't comfortable with having all my money tied up in it and wanted to get rid of it. He said he'd put an advert in the back of *Top Marques* for me. I was thinking, 'By the time that comes out and we've found a buyer for it I'll be in prison for non-payment of taxes.' I really couldn't wait that long. I suggested there might be someone in the trade who might be interested, and Mark warned me that I'd take quite a hit if I sold it through the trade rather than to a private buyer. I told him that was fine, I just wanted the money out, so he called a mate of his who owned a Ferrari dealership and came back to me with an offer of £55,000. I'd paid £80,000 for it, but it was only a week before my tax was due, so I accepted.

I was gutted. I was relieved because the tax bill was covered, but I was still gutted. Mark was right, I loved that car. I used to go up to his garages every day to polish it. I kept it immaculate. There wasn't a stone chip or a scuff or a ding anywhere on it. It really was my pride and joy, and just like that it was gone. I didn't even have anything in the bank to show for it. The two grand difference between what I got for the 360 and what I still needed to pay the taxman went towards the dealer's fees, so again I literally had nothing in the bank and was left driving my free Vauxhall Corsa.

A couple of months after the 360 went, Fiona called to say that Vauxhall wanted their car back; the deal was only for a year. So I didn't even have the Corsa now. I ended up buying yet another 1.9 Diesel Fiesta. My fourth second-hand Fiesta. I couldn't afford anything else. In what seemed like no time I'd gone from a brand-new Audi S4 to a beautiful black Ferrari 360 to a free Vauxhall Corsa to a second-hand Fiesta.

It was my own fault, I know that. For a start, I shouldn't have just given someone I hardly knew £55,000 to start a business, and I should have put a little aside to cover unexpected events. What I should have done and what I did, though, were two totally different things, and I paid for it with my dream car.

A Ferrari to a Fiesta in a matter of months. Kicks in the nuts don't come much harder than that.

Not that I've changed. I still spend every penny on cars, I still stretch myself thin, and sadly, yes, I still experience a moment of panic every time the taxman comes knocking, wondering if I've got enough to cover the bill, and if not, where the hell I'm going to get it from. It's just the way I am. People say you should always keep a little bit back, just in case. I never have. If I've got it, I spend it. On cars. Having spent several years with nothing, and sometimes less than that, I tend to treat everything as a bonus. The cars, my house – they're things I never thought I'd have in the first place, so I'm going to make the most of them while I can. I've never felt the need for security. I've never needed to know that I've got some cash stashed away under the mattress. Maybe that's because I know my mum's got a spare room in her house and she would always welcome me back with open arms. Maybe it's because I know I can always sell a car. If I need the money, I might have to take a bit of a hit, but I'll be able to get it. Whatever the case, I'll pick driving it over having it sitting in the bank every time.

25 CARS AND BOND GIRLS

I suppose I was a bit of a late starter when it came to women. Cars and cooking were my real passions; there wasn't a great deal of room for much else. By the time I was old enough to fully appreciate girls I was already flambéing chicken livers and obsessed with Ferraris, so, like music, they were a distraction I didn't really have time for. Though I used to fight with everyone else in my class at catering college for a place on the front bench, not because we wanted to be teacher's pet but because it afforded the best view of the girls on the beauty course coming and going across the car park, if a pretty girl and a good-looking car happened to be in that car park at the same time, the car would probably be the one attracting my gaze. Once I left college I was either too busy working or too broke to be able to afford a girlfriend, and though the money situation's improved over the years, the hours are still a bone of contention.

Not that I'm complaining. I've done all right, thanks

very much. Better than most, that's for sure, and better, some might argue, than a bloke from Yorkshire who's spent too much time with his head buried in a copy of *AutoTrader* could reasonably expect. Better still was when the ladies in question chased me. I'm not saying that women throw themselves at me, more that they give me a good kick to wake me up and get my attention. For reasons I've never been able to understand, my track record is full of head-strong women who, no doubt bored of waiting for me to notice them or to take the hint and ask them out, have taken the initiative and made the first move. Which is probably just as well: most of them were so obviously out of my league I wouldn't have given myself a chance.

It's probably fitting, then, that my longest relationship (at the time of writing at least) started without me even being in the room. I first met Barbara Broccoli, daughter of the legendary Bond producer 'Cubby' Broccoli and, with half-brother Michael G. Wilson, co-producer of the current James Bond films, after she won me, or at least my culinary skills, in a charity auction. She paid to have me cook a meal at her house in London, which came as quite a surprise as I didn't even know I was in the auction. A friend, or supposed friend of mine, David, who had been the head chef at the hotel on Park Lane where I first did work experience in London, had put me up for it. The auction was held at the Bournemouth Spa Hotel in aid of a local children's hospice; David had a restaurant in Bournemouth at the time and was somehow involved with the event. I vaguely remembered him mentioning something about it in passing at some gig we were doing, but you get asked to do a lot of things by a lot of people at demos and food festivals and I'm not sure I realised I was actually putting my name down for it. Either way, Barbara was there because one of the producers of the stage version of *Chitty Chitty Bang Bang*, which Barbara's production company EON was doing at the time, lived in Bournemouth and had invited her along. As I said, I was one of the lots, and Barbara won me (no doubt it was the spun sugar that swung it).

The first time we met was about six weeks later when I turned up at her place. It was a beautiful house in London, and the first thing I did when I got there was nearly burn it down. I put the grill on instead of the oven and didn't so much warm the bread as set fire to it. Not the best start, but she thought it was funny and it set the mood for the rest of the evening. Many of these types of events, especially if they take place in someone else's house, can be very formal, but this was really relaxed. It was just Barbara, five of her friends, and me and Gail, who'd worked at the Hotel Du Vin and was helping me out for the evening. We did four courses (minus bread) and a good time was had by all. I just remember getting in the car at the end of the evening, turning to Gail and saying that I thought Barbara was the most amazing woman I'd ever met. She was hilarious. The whole evening, start to finish, was hilarious. We just clicked. And the thing was, I didn't know anything about her. I didn't know who she was or what she did; I didn't know anything about the Bond set-up. I just thought she was an amazing woman.

Next day I told my PA at the time, Erica, all about the evening. I didn't know it at the time, but Erica got straight on the phone to Barbara's PA who then got together with some of Barbara's friends and between them they decided to play Cupid and set me up with her. And I, of course, fell for it. Erica told me that Barbara's PA was trying to organise a surprise for Barbara's birthday but didn't know what to do, so I offered to cook. Barbara's friends didn't tell her anything about it. She thought she was going to another charity dinner – she goes to a lot of charity dinners – but instead they stopped off at my place, and when she walked in I'd prepared this surprise meal for her. And that was it. After another equally hilarious evening we exchanged numbers, and thus began the most surreal, exciting and unforgettable four and a half years of my life.

Barbara was incredibly easy to be around. My phrase for her was 'Being with you is as easy as breathing,' and it was. She's a very loving, caring person, always worrying about other people and looking after them, never putting herself first. She's generous to a fault, too. She'd never ask for anything but would do everything to make you happy. Unlike a lot of the people in her business, she's not pretentious or ostentatious and when it was just the two of us she was the best company you could ask for.

She also happened to be one of the most powerful women in Hollywood. Not knowing much about her when we met, I didn't really have any concept of just how powerful she was. And Hollywood? Well, nothing can prepare you for it. It's insane, as are most of the people in it. It's no wonder they're all in and out of therapy and rehab like they're drop-in centres. Being involved in TV's crazy enough; being involved in film, even at a very basic level, is like being on another planet. At Barbara's level, it really is a different universe. As I said, I thought I was doing all right, a man still in his twenties who'd been a head chef and who owned a house and a nice motor, who'd written books and been invited to celebrity parties (though I never went). I thought I knew what success was, until I met Barbara. After we got together, I wasn't just moving in different circles, it was like I'd suddenly been blasted into outer space and arrived in another dimension where all the super famous, super powerful people lived.

'Another dimension' is really the only way to describe the US film industry. It's a hyper-reality. There aren't many normal people in it, just very shiny ones. And the money involved is stupid. Once I went to a car launch at the Dorchester with Barbara which Toyota had put on especially for her. They wanted to get one of their new cars in the next Bond film and were offering to pay for the pleasure. To help convince her, they did a huge launch, just for her and the Bond team – smoke, lasers, a spinning stage. The bigwigs of Toyota had flown over for it. The whole thing must have cost hundreds of thousands. They needn't have bothered though. Barbara asked me to come with her because she knew nothing much about cars and wanted my opinion, and when they pulled back the cover she got it instantly. I can't remember what car it was, but it wasn't great. Getting a product in a Bond film is a major coup for a company, potentially worth millions to them, and these are the kinds of lengths they're willing to go to to impress people. She's a powerful woman all right.

It wasn't until the first time I went to LA that I realised Barbara was in a different league. We'd been together a while. She had to go there on business and she called me to ask if I wanted to join her. Having never been to America, I jumped at the chance. She organised everything. I should have twigged that this wasn't going to be your average trip when she sent a car to pick me up from home and take me to the airport. When I got to Heathrow I was standing at the back of a long, snaking queue at the BA check-in desk when this woman came up to me and said, 'Can I see your ticket please, sir? Yes, I think you might be in the wrong queue. Will you follow me please, sir?' I was thinking I was going to be arrested or something as I followed her round the corner and into this other area, but it turned out to be the first-class lounge. There had to be some mistake. No, she assured me I had a first-class ticket and that I should make myself at home. I'd only walked round the corner but already I was in another world, all sofas and champagne bars. I called my mother. 'You're never going to believe this, I'm in first class.' And it really was amazing. I had a bed on the flight and everything. I couldn't believe it. I'd never experienced anything like it before in my life. I was taking pictures of absolutely everything, and that was just on the plane.

When I landed at LA airport there was a guy with a sign saying 'Mr Martin' waiting in arrivals. I followed him outside to a limousine, got in the back, and off we went to Beverly Hills. And that's when it all just went really nuts.

It was about a 20-minute drive from the airport to Barbara's house. We were driving along the 405 San Diego Freeway, on to Wilshire, left on to Santa Monica Boulevard and past the 'Welcome to Beverly Hills' sign. The sun was blazing, there were palm trees everywhere, and I was sat in the back of a limo thinking it couldn't get any better than this. Then we pulled up at the house. This house was beautiful. I walked into a huge hallway with a spiral stair-case, rooms leading off it in every direction. The lounge was twice the size of my place. There was a swimming pool out back and more guest quarters … it seemed endless. I was barely able to take it all in. 'What am I doing here?' I kept thinking. 'How did this happen?' It was a stunning place – or it was until I walked into the garage where she had not one but two Volvos, a saloon *and* an estate. Barbara will only drive Volvos because they're the safest cars on the road – although the way most Volvo drivers drive it's everyone else on the road who needs to worry. But then that's Barbara. Even in the middle of all the glamour of Beverly Hills she's still down to earth and practical.

We spent a couple of days just chilling at the house, then Barbara had to get back to work, which was going to leave me at a bit of a loose end, especially as I didn't really know the place or anyone there, but I was quite happy to just relax by the pool and enjoy the sun and some time off. So she headed off to work one morning and I was lounging around the house when I heard the doorbell. Actually, the house was so big it took me a while to work out where the ringing was coming from. It rang again. I continued to wander around, trying to track down the noise. Finally I found my way to the hall and opened the door to a guy immaculately dressed in a black suit, white shirt and tie, and in his hand he was holding a silver plate with an envelope and my name, 'J. Martin Esq.', on it. He smiled, showing perfect white teeth, and said, 'Welcome to Beverly Hills, sir.' I opened the envelope and inside was a little note from Barbara – 'Enjoy Beverly Hills, I'll see you later, love B' – and a set of car keys with a prancing horse on the fob. I looked at the guy, he smiled at me again, said, 'Enjoy Beverly Hills,' then turned round and walked off. And sat there on the drive was a red Ferrari 360 Spyder, exactly the same as the black 360 I used to have but with a soft top, which, let's face it, you've got to have in Beverly Hills.

With that the phone rang. It was Barbara checking that I'd got it.

'Yeah, I've got it,' I replied, 'but what am I supposed to do with it?'

'Well,' she said, 'you're on the insurance, just go for a drive.'

Ten minutes later, with the top down, I was driving through the perfectly manicured streets of Beverly Hills. I swung left on to Rodeo and just cruised along, It was un-believable. A few days earlier I was in my little house in Winchester, now I was in a Ferrari 360 – red, cream leather, top down – driving down Rodeo Drive. Insane. As I drove down Sunset Boulevard I called a mate of mine, Pippa's fella Steve, and said, 'You're not going to believe this, mate. I'm driving a Ferrari 360 along the Sunset Strip.'

I drove all over the place that day, up and down the Strip and right over to Malibu, just taking it all in. Then I had a brainwave. I thought, 'Nobody knows me here, nobody knows I'm a chef, I'm going to go to KFC.' So I drove to a KFC drive-thru in my shiny red drop-top Ferrari and got myself a bargain bucket. Now that's what you call surreal.

The second time I went to the States with Barbara it was to New York for Christmas. She has a magnificent house there, which, like her house in the UK, I almost burnt down the minute I set foot in it. Well, I didn't, but the fire department didn't know that until they'd turned up at the door wanting to know where the fire was.

I had woken up really early one morning wanting a bacon butty, one made with that ace American bacon. It was only a bit of bacon so I didn't bother putting the extractor fan on – I didn't want to wake everyone with the noise. The next thing I knew there were sirens outside, and when I looked out of the window to see what was going on I saw six 38 foot laddered fire trucks, big blokes with axes piling out of them, heading straight for Barbara's front door. I opened the door, bacon sandwich in hand, and this fireman shouted, 'Where's the fire?' With all the commotion everybody else in the house had now woken up and they were all coming down in their dressing gowns and asking what was going on. Butty still in hand, I told them that apparently there was a fire in the house. The fireman insisted that a silent smoke alarm in the kitchen had been triggered, and with that he barged through, only to find a dirty frying pan and an open pack of bacon.

'Ah,' I said. 'I think that might have been me.'

A week or so later we went to a New Year party out of town. The thing I remember most of all about that day was the horrendous journey, how nuts it was. The trip over there was just unbearable. I got really wound up because I always like to know where I'm going and the driver hadn't got a clue. He got so lost, and we were in this big Cadillac with these awful bench seats, and every time we went round a corner we all slid along this bloody seat. I hate modern American cars at the best of times but Barbara and the kids were pissing themselves laughing, sliding all over the place, while I was just getting more and more hacked off.

When we eventually got to this place it was an amazing house, owned by a famous composer. The party was in full swing, caterers and staff running around everywhere. Barbara introduced me to the owner and we got on straight away, same sense of humour and everything. I really liked him and thought he was very funny. But he was totally mad, completely off his rocker, the type of person who really doesn't give a shit, which is hilarious, unless you're on the receiving end of it. But I thought he was great, and it was a great party, mayhem everywhere: dogs running around, kids running around, people and noise every-where.

At one point I slipped off into another room to call my mum and wish her a happy new year. I was sat in this beautiful lounge overlooking the ocean, there was a fabulous big black piano by the window, and next to me a display cabinet which covered the entire left-hand side of the room and was absolutely heaving with Oscars, Baftas, Golden Globes, Grammys, you name it. I have a clear memory of being on the phone to my mother, wishing her a happy new year, with an Oscar in my hand, looking out of the window and being absolutely awestruck by the ocean view.

I know this all sounds weird, but everything about that time in my life really was unbelievable. I went to the Baftas one year. Barbara never did the whole red carpet bit so we went in the back way. She never did anything in front of cameras because she doesn't enjoy having her photograph taken. We went straight to our seats, alongside lots of important industry people – the producers, the studio bosses, the money men. I remember Harvey Weinstein of Miramax was there. Everyone thinks that actors are the most important people in Hollywood. They're not. They're the employees, and these guys are their bosses.

As we waited for the show to begin, we watched what was going on on the red carpet on the big screen at the front of the stage. All the actors and actresses outside were doing their bit, posing for photographs, signing autographs and waving to fans, and then a minute later we would see them walk through the doors into the auditorium, which was weird enough in itself. Oscar-winning actress and new Bond girl (as she was then) Halle Berry was one of them, and when she came through the auditorium doors she walked up the centre aisle, came down my row and sat next to me. She turned round to Barbara, who for some reason was sitting behind me, and said, 'Hi B, how ya doin'?' Then she turned to me. 'Hey James, how's it goin'?'

I'm like, sorry? What? Me?

While I was trying to get my head round that one, Nicole Kidman sat down in front of me. She too turned round. 'Hi Barb, hi James.' It was just ridiculous.

As soon as the lights went down and the show started I was there with my phone, trying to be all subtle, texting my mates: Halle Berry and Nicole Kidman just asked how I was doing.

Barbara leant forward. 'What are you doing?'

'Nothing, just checking to see if I've got any messages.'

And then I found myself at the after-show party and all these faces I recognised, mega famous people, were coming up to Barbara and chatting, shaking my hand, saying it's nice to meet you, and you know that they're just normal people, but it's the hardest thing to get your head around. Back home I was used to meeting famous people, yet still I was starstruck.

You see, as fun as these events were, I always felt like a small fish in a very big pond. If she wasn't away filming, scouting locations or meeting actors, actresses and directors, Barbara was forever being invited to this or that. There was always a dinner or a party to go to, and it was business so it went with the job. But I always felt out of my depth, a bit like a spare part. I think Barbara knew that because she would always check I was okay, that I was being looked after, that I was having a good time and, when she could, she'd do her best to engineer it so that I had someone to talk to.

Most people involved in the film industry, especially the ones you meet at parties, are self-obsessed lunatics who either talk about themselves constantly or are in the loo snorting anything they can get their hands on, so most of the time I'd rather have been at home watching TV, but I did have one great conversation with a guy at the Baftas party. Barbara very specifically sat me next to him, and within about five minutes I knew why. He never mentioned food or what I did for a living, and I didn't know what he did, we just talked non-stop all evening about cars. There was all this pomp and circumstance going on around us, and Barbara was networking, but we were just chatting away about this Ferrari and that Aston, motors we'd owned, cars we'd like to own. It was only in the car on the way home that Barbara told me he was the CEO of Sony.

Cars are a great leveller. I think that's why me and Daniel Craig always got on. Whenever we got together that's all we talked about. We were sat opposite each other at this dinner at Nobu one night and we just chatted away about motors. Daniel was about to be given the keys to the Aston Martin DBS – it comes with the job: all the Bonds are given an Aston Martin – and he was really excited because we'd both been to Aston Martin's HQ at Gaydon to see it and it looked amazing. We were talking about how excited he was when Barbara turned to us and laughed.

'It's always about cars with you two,' she said. 'Haven't you got anything else to talk about?'

To which I replied, 'What do you want us to talk about, bloody Bond?'

To be fair, we did talk a bit about Bond. These were exciting times for Daniel, his life was about to change for ever. I don't think he realised just how much. We used to talk a bit about food and cooking too. But mainly it was about cars.

When we went to Gaydon to see that DBS for the first time, the pair of us were like kids in a sweet shop. This was the Aston Martin Daniel drove in *Casino Royale*, but we went to see it when it was just a clay model, before they'd actually built any. Again, it was another of these big pitches, looking for Barbara's approval. If they didn't get it, if the car didn't make it into the film, the chances were it would never be more than a lump of clay. Barbara wanted me to go and have a look at it with her, so we drove up there, met Daniel, and went into this meeting with all the bigwigs, including Aston Martin boss Ulrich Betz. A cover was pulled off to reveal this full-size clay model spray-painted to look exactly as the finished car would. It was all top secret. No one but the people in the room had even seen a drawing of this thing, let alone what we were seeing, so no cameras or phones were allowed in the building – except for Barbara of course. She could do whatever she liked and was there taking pictures from every angle.

'It's all right that, isn't it?' Daniel said to me. 'What do you think?'

'That's fucking ace,' I said. 'It looks the bollocks.'

You could tell it was going to be a seriously amazing bit of kit. Even as a model it looked incredible.

Barbara soon finished taking her pictures – her interest was purely professional and she'd seen what she needed to see – but me and Daniel were still all over it, so she said she'd go and get some lunch and leave us to it. Of course, when she got back we were still there looking at it. The detail was incredible. They had mock-ups of the interior and all the Bond gadgets that were going to go on it – the defibrillator, the champagne holder in the back. Then they started arguing over the colour. They had these mock-up boards with different colours on and one of the guys from Aston was saying that he thought it should be graphite, like a gun-metal grey. Barbara turned to me and asked, 'What colour do you think it should be, James?'

Now that was surreal. I was being asked what colour I thought the new Bond car should be. Everyone knows that Bond's Aston's got to be silver. The graphite was too grey; it needed to be lighter. On the other hand you don't want a silver that's too white otherwise it'll just look rubbish. We went through the colour chart that displayed the different grades of silver and found the perfect one. Barbara turned to the Aston guy and said, 'We'll have that one then.' So there you go, if you didn't like the colour of the DBS in *Casino Royale*, you can blame me (only joking!).

And as if that wasn't enough for one day, just when we thought it couldn't possibly get any better, Ulrich Betz asked me and Daniel if we were ready for a test drive, and which car did we want to go out in first, the new DB9 Sport or an immaculate 1964 platinum DB5 formerly owned by George Harrison? Daniel and I just looked at each other, unable to decide which to go for first. Barbara was laughing and rolling her eyes at us for being like eight-year-olds who've just been told they can have any toy in the toy shop. Luckily there was no choice to be made as we got a go in both, Daniel in the DB5 first and me in the DB9 Sport, blatting it around the Gaydon test track accompanied by racing drivers whose sole purpose seemed to be to tell us to drive 'faster' and really 'push it', which we happily did. The funny thing was, this was at a time when the tabloids were really opposed to Daniel being the new James Bond and were running all these ridiculous stories about him, including one that he couldn't drive. As anyone who saw him going round the track at Gaydon in the DB5 would know, that allegation is a load of bollocks.

In the four and a half years Barbara and I were together there were many strange and exciting Bond-related moments. I watched the ice hotel in *Die Another Day* melt right in front of me. I accidentally knocked the very first script for *Casino Royale* off the counter in her kitchen and only noticed when my dog Fudge had pulled it apart and reshuffled the pages like a pack of cards; I then spent a whole flight to New York frantically trying to put these unnumbered pages back in order before delivering it to her, who again, luckily, saw the funny side. I even babysat *Casino Royale* Bond girl Eva Green's yappy little dog in Venice while she and Daniel were sailing up and down the

Grand Canal in a fabulous yacht. But of all the Bond moments, nothing came close to that day with Daniel at Gaydon. Like Barbara said, 'It's always about cars.'

26 JAGS, RANGES, BIKES AND BOATS

The one thing I can never get my head around is the fact that the more successful you become and the more money you make, the more people want to give you things. Or they do if you're on TV. I'd already experienced it with my discounted kitchen and Vauxhall Corsa. However, when Jaguar called and asked if I wanted to be part of their VIP scheme, I knew that this was a different league. The VIP scheme wasn't actually free, but with only a monthly subscription covering tax and insurance, it was as good as. I didn't go looking for it either. I'd done a couple of photo shoots with the 360, mentioned in a couple of interviews that I liked cars, and next thing I knew I was being offered cars that I'd gladly have paid for. Jaguar would invite a personality from each area of sport and entertainment to drive their cars. They had a golfer, a cricketer and a rugby player and they were looking for a chef who was young, well known and fitted whatever marketing profile they had. You paid your monthly fee and for that they gave you a new car every few months and covered all costs except petrol.

I had five Jaguars in total before moving to Range Rover's VIP scheme, and I drove four of their top-of-the-range models. There was no more commitment involved than driving the cars. You'd get invited to polo matches and various other events but there was no obligation to go. I can't stand all that nonsense so I never went, and no one ever suggested I should. There were no photo shoots, no adverts, no appearances or plugs in interviews, they were just happy to know that people were seeing you drive their car. At least they were until they suddenly 'closed' the scheme and asked for their Range Rover back. Call me a cynic, but being asked to hand the keys back just happened to coincide with Gordon and Jamie becoming household names. Suddenly they were driving Range Rovers and I wasn't. But perhaps we all just shared the same taste in cars.

While I was still VIP enough to be a member of these schemes, I couldn't fault the service. When I first met Barbara I had an S Type, then as soon as we got together I was unexpectedly upgraded to a fabulous XKR – this was when Jaguar had just paid to get the XKR into *Die Another Day*. It was a fantastic car, a black convertible with mega alloy wheels. It was just beautiful, one of the few cars I've had that my mum completely fell in love with. Thankfully, Jaguar's customer service was highly accommodating and amazingly understanding when those mega alloys got nicked one night. That they were nicked outside Barbara's house might have had some bearing on how they reacted to the news that I'd come down in the morning to find their car lying on the ground with all four wheels gone. After literally dragging it off the road and onto a trailer, and telling me not to worry about it, it wasn't a problem, these things happen, they delivered an identical replacement two days later. Now that's service.

One of the other benefits of being part of VIP schemes was that I didn't have to spend any money on cars. My biggest expense simply wasn't there any more. This was when I started to get into bikes and boats. And we're not talking a BMX and a rubber dinghy here.

My first bike was what you might call an impulse buy. I'd been shopping in Southampton with Pippa, my PA, and on the way back I stopped off at Harley Davidson for something to eat because they do the best burgers anywhere. The burger bar is actually right in the middle of the showroom, so we were sitting there eating our burger and fries and looking at all the great bikes around us when I spotted this mega Fatboy, a big black thing with solid wheels that looked just like the one Arnie drove in *Terminator*. For the rest of the meal I couldn't take my eyes off it. Once I'd finished eating I wandered over to give it a once-over, had a sit on it, and this guy Darren, who became a great friend of mine over the years (he sadly passed away recently – you are missed, mate), came over and started to tell me all about it. Then he fired it up, and 15 minutes later I'd bought the thing.

There were, however, two snags. One was that I had nowhere to put my new toy, even though I'd moved out of the two-bedroom flat in Winchester High Street, which had turned into a bit of nightmare. As soon as I started to get recognised as that bloke off the TV people began to shout up at my windows and through my letterbox. Usually it was just drunken nonsense from pissed-up lads staggering down the high street after closing time on a Friday or Saturday night, but when those same lads started to think it was funny to piss through my letterbox while they were shouting their abuse, I decided it was time to find somewhere else to live. I moved into a converted Baptist chapel on the outskirts of Winchester. It was a lovely two-bedroom place, but though the house itself gave me a bit more floor space, I still didn't have a garage and there wasn't any room to build one, so my mean black *Terminator* bike ended up in the middle of the conservatory.

The other snag was that I couldn't actually ride it. I'd mucked about on bikes as a kid, hoofing it about the farm on my little Puch 50, but I'd never actually got a motorbike licence. So, for the next three months the Fatboy remained a very expensive, albeit very cool, ornament. Sitting there looking at this ace motorbike night after night, I began to get increasingly frustrated at not being able to ride it. In the end it got too much and I decided to go and do my bike test.

Typically, I managed to pick the wettest day since records began to do it. It was absolutely chucking it down with rain, the worst possible conditions to be going out on a bike full stop, never mind trying to pass a test. I got to the test centre and walked into a waiting room full of 17- and 18-year-old boys and girls, all sitting there crying their eyes out. Literally, every single one of them was in tears. The examiner came through, introduced himself and as we were walking outside said, 'I should warn you that no one has passed their test today.' They'd all hit the brakes and come straight off apparently, because it was so wet. Obviously that didn't fill me with confidence.

Then, just to make life even more uncomfortable, once we were on our bikes the examiner came on the intercom and said, 'Before we start, do you know a girl called Clare Brewer?'

I was already nervous about the test, and I wasn't really sure where this might go, so I told him, 'I think I might know her. I don't really remember.'

'Yes you do,' he insisted. 'Clare Brewer. She worked at a hotel with you. You went out with her for a few weeks.'

'Oh yes, yes, I remember Clare,' I said.

'Well, I'm her dad. Shall we get going?'

I was nervous enough as it was, and being confronted with an ex-girlfriend's dad didn't help. I sat there on the bike thinking, 'Well, that's it then, I've failed already. Might as well get off now.' But after 15 minutes of driving through the most torrential rain I've ever seen in my life, he told me he'd seen enough and I'd passed.

That at least meant I could now ride the Fatboy instead of just look at it. I still didn't have anywhere sensible to put it though, so it stayed as the centrepiece of the conservatory for quite a while after that.

I enjoyed riding a bike so much that a week after passing my test I went out and bought a Ducati for the conservatory too, and since then I've had a Harley Davidson V Rod, a

My average weekend! Emptying the garage before trying to fit more in ...
Lucky I've got a big drive!

The first mode of transport I was allowed to drive. One careful owner.

This is just one of the many *Mail on Sunday* toys I get to play with!

The first thing any bloke buys himself when he gets a garden. I won't let anyone else do the mowing, even the gardener – I love driving this thing!

I love F1 cars, but never thought some day I would own some. Driving them is like no other experience on earth.

Track days are great fun, if only to thrash somebody else's car.

Groupie, I know, but I just had to – he's a hero of mine. Mr Moss, you're a legend.

Me and Sarah, all dressed and ready for the off. Three hours until the start of the greatest road race in the world!

How much is it gonna cost me if I crash this thing?

30 years of working my arse off for this moment!

If only I'd joined the 'Wanna be a racing driver?' queue at the school career fair, then I could do this for a living.

Cool hat or what? Me, I mean – Sarah looks a bit like the crazy frog! Jokes aside, this was the realisation of my dream and worth every drop of sweat, blood and tears.

Ducati 999, a Wurtz Custom Chopper, a Yamaha Raptor 700R Quad and three mopeds. You could say I got bitten quite badly by the motorbike bug, all because Pippa and I stopped off for a burger and chips on the way back from the shops and I had a bit of spare cash because I wasn't spending it all on cars.

Honestly, me having spare money is lethal. I haven't even banked the cheque before I feel it burning a hole in my pocket. No wonder my financial adviser is always trying to tie every penny he can get his hands on into 15-year investment plans. The thing is, as much as I always spend it – and it is true that when I get offered a job I don't think about what it will do for my bank balance but what it will do for my garage – in a roundabout way even the craziest of purchases seems to end up being profitable and good for business. When I had the Westfield and the Caterham, for instance, I used to get loads of attention, and I swear that they did my image the world of good and made me a far more exciting option in the eyes of some TV people I was meeting at the time. I'm not saying I got the work because I turned up to the studio in an open-top two-seater track car, but they certainly remembered me. And if it hadn't been for my well-known love of cars I'd never have got my motoring column in the *Mail on Sunday*, Jaguar and Range Rover would never have invited me to join their VIP schemes and I'd never have had the spare cash needed to get into boats, which despite costing an ungodly amount of cash in the end proved to be one of the biggest money spinners.

It was Mark Papworth who first introduced me to the

Bladerunner 34GT. The name says it all. A £120,000, 100 mph race-spec powerboat, 34 feet long, red and white, two seats – it looked like a drug runner's boat, like something out of *Miami Vice*. Really, if we're being honest, it did just look like a huge penis. Mark took me down to Southampton to meet this mate of his who built them. We went out on the water in one, just for a bit of fun; three and a half minutes later we hit the Isle of Wight. That's how fast this thing was. Practically the whole thing was out of the water, flying along, skimming the waves. It had a racing hull and a cockpit based on an F16 fighter. It was basically a Ferrari on water, only it had a flatscreen TV, a Playstation 2 and a DVD player in the back. By the time we got back from the Isle of Wight I'd already made up my mind. I was having one.

I knew nothing about boats and I'd always hated the idea of sailing. I couldn't be bothered with tacking and sails and taking all afternoon to travel 5 miles. I don't do knots either. This was different though. After a quick training course in Portsmouth I was ready to go. I used to finish *Ready Steady Cook*, jump on the Fatboy and hoof it back to Winchester. Me, Pippa and Pippa's fella Steve would then get in the car, pop to M&S and get a load of sandwiches and picnic food, and by seven o'clock we'd be pottering down the river to the coast ready to blat it over to the Isle of Wight. On a beautiful sunny day it was unbelievable, the best experience you'll ever have in your life. We'd moor up in a lovely harbour area and it would be so relaxing. It was just what I needed at the time because it was manic at work. To be out on the water away from everything, or bobbing up and down in a harbour, was perfect.

The only downside was that when you pulled into a harbour you were suddenly with all these other 'boaties', and I never really got on with 'boaties'. Most of them were old guys who spent all day knocking back the gin in their enormous triple-decker floating palaces, surrounded by girls who looked young enough to be their daughters. Whoever had the biggest boat was the best. I couldn't be bothered with all that. I just liked chopping through the waves at 100 miles an hour. I didn't want to talk about cleats and hull sizes with these people. And anyway, it didn't matter how big your gin palace was, nothing beat that Bladerunner. Red and sleek, it was always the coolest boat in the water. And the noise it used to make when you throttled it up was phenomenal. It was mad, but so much fun.

It was also stupidly expensive. My boat was called 2XS, and in every way it was. Ashley Levett, one of the investors in the Hotel Du Vin, once said to me that when it comes to owning boats, the two best days of your life are the day you buy it and the day you sell it; everything else is a nightmare. And he was right. The day I bought it was unbelievable, at all other times I was aware of just how astronomically expensive it was. Every month I'd write a cheque for two grand, and that was just for mooring, purely to have it sat down in Southampton. Insurance was a small fortune every year. On top of that, the boat wasn't anti-foulled, which means the hull hadn't been painted with this special copper coating to stop fungi and green algae sticking to it, because I wanted a polished hull so that the boat would go quicker. Every ten days the boat had to be lifted out of the water on a crane, jet-washed, then put back in the water again. Every lift was £240. That's £240 to take it out of the water and another £240 to put it back in the water. The jet-washing part was free, and so it bloody well should have been. So altogether it was over £2,600 every month, and that's before you went anywhere in it. To fill it up with fuel for a day out was another grand.

Towards the end of my two years of boating I was spending more and more time with Barbara in London and less and less time making like Crockett and Tubbs. I was still writing the cheques but having less and less time to enjoy it, so reluctantly I decided to sell it.

Before I sold it, though, the company that built it asked me if they could use it for the Southampton Boat Show. In exchange for a free service I agreed to let them use it on the stand. The organisers of the boat show then got wind of the fact that my boat was going to be there and they got in touch and said that they fancied having a restaurant at the show, would I be interested in running it for them? I went down there, did a bit of a recce, and said, 'Why not?' They asked how much I wanted for doing it and I said, 'Nothing. You can sort me out with a jet-ski instead.' They were happy with that, and I got a three-seater jet-ski, so I was happy too.

It was an 800-seater restaurant, which was just as well because in addition to all the visitors coming in for something to eat all the big bosses from these boat companies came in to have meetings. On the second day I was wandering around the restaurant, checking that everything was all right, and this guy from P&O introduced himself and gave me his card, saying that he'd love to work with me. I was thinking, 'P&O? Ferries? I don't think so.' But three weeks later I got a call from him inviting me to come down and look at this new cruise liner they were working on, and I accepted.

When I got to Southampton, before I'd even walked up the gang plank, I'd decided it wasn't really for me: the place was full of old people with walking frames. So I said to the P&O guy, 'Mate, before you show me any more, I'm really not interested.' But he was very insistent. He told me that they were working on a new concept: cruises for people who don't do cruises. The age bracket was going to be cut in half, it was all going to be much cooler and more stylish, and they really wanted to have a James Martin Bistro on board. After about two weeks of talking over ideas and looking at plans and drawings and artist's impressions, he finally convinced me that it was a good idea.

The boat was *Ocean Village*, and it was an instant hit. It turned out to be one of the most popular boats in P&O's fleet, and the restaurant was absolutely heaving. *Ocean Village Two* followed four years later, and me and my chef Chris split our time between the two, cruising around the Mediterranean and the Caribbean.

It is quite surreal really. All my work in some way or another relates to motors. Jaguar gave me a free car, and a series of motorbikes, one powerboat and a jet-ski later I ended up with two hugely successful restaurants. I'm sure my financial adviser didn't think a red and white 100 mph Bladerunner was such a good use for my money at the time (and when I was writing cheques left, right and centre neither did I), but in the end it more than paid for itself. And it was bloody good fun.

27 MY FIRST OLDIE: THE GULLWING

I have a habit of going into places to buy one thing and coming out with another. Like the time I went to the German Motor Show in Essen with a Pagani Zonda super-car on my mind and came home the proud owner of a vintage (1955) Mercedes-Benz 300SL Gullwing. And not just any old Gullwing, one of the best examples in the world.

Having reluctantly sold my *Miami Vice* drug runner, and still being on a VIP scheme, I had a bit of spare cash and was looking for something exciting to do with it. The Pagani Zonda seemed to fit the bill exactly. It looked like the Batmobile, had rockets for exhausts and not a lot of boot space, and as Italian supercars go it was pretty extreme. At £225,000 it wasn't cheap, but it was half the price of a Ferrari Enzo and looked like it might be just as much fun. I'd seen one at Mark Papworth's garages. Another guy who stored cars with him had a 1980s 288GTO Ferrari, a Lamborghini Miura (like the one Rossano Brazzi drove up the mountain at the start of the original *The Italian Job*) and the first right-hand-drive Pagani Zonda in the country, silver with blue interior, the absolute mutt's nuts. He'd had it for about a year, he was going to sell it, and I wanted to buy it. But this car was a hell of a lot of money, not far off what I'd paid for my house, which I still had a large mortgage on, so I thought I'd take time to have a good long think about things before I did anything.

I was flicking through a car magazine one day and came across a piece about the Essen Motor Show, which said it was the greatest car show in the world. I asked Mark if he fancied shooting over there for a quick look, maybe help me make my mind up about the Zonda while we were at it. It's not that far so we drove over there; from Calais to Essen is about 260 miles, and on a good run you can do it in just under three hours, and you get to hoof it on the autobahn. I'd never been to Germany anyway so it was a good excuse to get over there and have a drive.

When we got there it turned out that the magazine hadn't really done the event justice. It was double the size of any motor show I'd ever been to and it had the best of everything, vintage and modern, but mostly vintage. You needed three days to get round it, it was that huge. As we walked in, the first thing we saw was the Mercedes-Benz stand. In pride of place they had the brand-new SLR McLaren, which had literally only just come out, and next to that two Gullwings side by side. Instantly Mark and I felt drawn to them, beautiful silver cars with red leather interiors.

The salesman, a guy called Ulrich, popped the hood on

one of them and we stared at its pristine engine. Then he said, 'Would you like to sit in it?' Would I? Too bloody right I would. The door was already up so I slid into the car's sumptuous interior – red leather, chrome switches, ivory steering wheel. Surrounded by this intoxicating vintage luxury I could feel myself falling in love with it. I got almost instantly high on the old-fashioned glamour of it and desperately tried to work out what €240,000 translated to in real money. Mark phoned his wife to check the exchange rate, she looked it up on the internet, and it worked out to be about £175,000.

Now, I'd just been looking at Pagani Zondas at £225,000, so suddenly £175,000 seemed very reasonable.

I'd never owned a classic car before in my life. I knew less than nothing about them. I'd never driven one, I'd never even sat in one. The only thing I knew about this 1955 Gullwing was that it was just beautiful.

I turned to my right and saw the salesman putting a sold sign, 'Verkauft', on the other Gullwing next to me. It was the first day of the show and it couldn't have been open more than ten minutes. The salesman came back over to me and he was being very courteous and attentive, like nothing I was used to. Prior to this, salesmen always used to look at me like I was about to nick something. I was only in a T-shirt and jeans – it wasn't like I'd dressed up for the occasion.

'Do you like it?' he asked.

'Oh yeah,' I replied. 'I like it a lot.'

Then he said something else which I didn't really hear.

I just nodded and said 'Yeah' again. The next minute he was putting another sold sign up, in the window of the Gullwing I was sitting in. He explained that I didn't have to buy it, but that as I was interested he'd put the sold sign on it and I could then fly out the following week, test-drive it, and if I liked it I could buy it. If I didn't, there was no obligation. No deposit or credit card number was required, my word was enough.

So I'd put my name down, albeit semi-accidentally, for the Gullwing, but the Pagani Zonda was still on my mind. That night in the hotel bar I was talking to Mark about it and he said that actually the Zonda was a bit too much of a footballer's car for his taste (true), whereas the Gullwing was classier (also true), and it was an absolutely iconic car.

The following day as we walked around I noticed that of the twelve Gullwings we'd seen the day before, dotted around the show, every single one had a sold sticker on it. There were lots of classic cars – Ferraris, Lamborghinis, Maseratis – and a lot were sold, but only the Gullwing had sold out. Which started me thinking that not only was this a beautiful car I'd be more than happy to own, it could actually be a really good buy.

All the way back to the UK Mark and I discussed the Gullwing, me wondering if buying it would be doing the right thing. As soon as I was home I was on the internet trying to do some research on the car. I still didn't really know anything about it. I didn't know if it was particularly rare, or if £175,000 was a good price. I stayed up all night trying to rectify that. I learned that while I wouldn't be paying over the odds for it, it was top whack, but then again it was mint condition and I was buying it from the Mercedes-Benz Classic Centre. It was never going to be a bargain, but it did come with great provenance, and I knew that the comprehensive restoration work that had been done on it would just about be the best.

The show finished on the Sunday and, with typical German efficiency, Mercedes-Benz phoned me first thing Monday morning to arrange the flights. They e-mailed me the tickets, and I flew over to Stuttgart with Mark and Pippa. We were collected from the airport in a vintage white Mercedes limo and taken straight to the Classic Centre. Ulrich met us there and told us that everything was ready for our test drive. They wheeled the car out, a racing driver got into the driver's seat, I got into the passenger seat, and we drove off up this mountain. This was a 50-year-old car but he was really driving it. He didn't take it gently up this steep road, he really floored it, and the Gullwing was making the most amazing noise. At the top the driver got out; now it was my turn. It was magic to drive, but really heavy, not what I was used to at all. Then again it wouldn't be. I'd never driven a 50-year-old car before.

When we got back I was all excited – kid-in-a-sweet-shop stuff again.

'What do you think?' Ulrich asked me.

'Yeah, I love it,' I replied. 'What happens now?'

He told me that if I left them a deposit I could wire them the rest in my own time and they'd then arrange delivery. So I wrote him a cheque. He reached out, shook my hand

and said, 'Congratulations, the car is yours.' Then he gave me all the bits and pieces that went with it: a car cover, booklets and, most importantly, the original sales brochure.

They treated me unbelievably well. Once the deal was done it wasn't the usual 'thanks very much and see you later', instead the relationship seemed to move up a notch to a whole new level. Ulrich proceeded to take me, Mark and Pippa on a guided tour of the place, where they were working on one of Ralph Lauren's cars from his private Mercedes-Benz car collection. He rolled up another shutter to reveal F1 cars, touring cars, Le Mans cars, Princess Diana's Mercedes – the place must have been 20,000 square feet and it was full of priceless cars. He approached one car, pulled back the cover, and it was Stirling Moss's legendary '722' Mille Miglia-winning SLR, the Holy Grail of motor sport and probably the most expensive car in the world. You couldn't put a price on that car, and me, Pippa and Mark were just stood there gawping at it.

'Sit in it,' Ulrich said.

It was like being a child again, back in that garage at Castle Howard, sitting in that Ferrari 308. I was almost too scared to touch anything. And then Ulrich leaned over, flicked the switch and fired it up. The noise! Unbelievable. I'd never heard anything like it.

Two weeks later I was at home, sitting by the phone, waiting for Mark to call because the car was being delivered straight to his garages. The second Mark called, I was in my car hoofing it over there. I arrived just as the lorry got there. Steve was there too. The three of us watched as the

Gullwing was wheeled down the ramps and off the trailer.

BANG! The ramp gave way and the car fell straight down. Its underside smacked the road, taking the exhaust off and denting the rear axle. For a split second we all just stood there in utter silence, staring at it, no one wanting to be the first to move or say anything. Next thing I was on the phone to Ulrich telling him that his delivery driver had just dropped my beautiful 1955 mint condition 300SL Gullwing off the back of the trailer and straight on to the floor. Ulrich was super apologetic and assured me he'd sort it. Before we knew it, the car was being loaded back on to the trailer and taken back to Germany.

Three weeks later it was back again, only this time not only did it have a new exhaust and axle, it had a load of upgrades on it too, including a two-grand radio, by way of an apology. All good. It made it off the trailer in one piece, and then it was sent off to be MOTed.

It failed. The brakes. I was back on the phone to Ulrich. He was super apologetic again and assured me he'd get an engineer straight out to me.

I was pulling my hair out by now. Remember, this was my first experience of classic cars. I know now that this kind of thing is par for the course, but at the time I couldn't believe it. Stressed doesn't quite cover how I was feeling, but it didn't last long. Within two hours a Mercedes mechanic turned up – a proper one too, not some kid on an apprenticeship – he sorted it all out, it went back to be MOTed in the afternoon, and thankfully it passed.

As soon as I was back behind the wheel, out for that

first awesome drive, gunning it through the New Forest, I realised what a mega, mega car I'd got myself.

A couple of weeks later, I went back to Chewton Glen to cater a dinner party for them. I do it every year, a charity dinner for 80 people, and one of the guests was my old manager from the Hotel Du Vin, who you will recall had once told me to choose between my TV career and the hotel. We hadn't seen each other since parting company several years earlier. He arrived in a brand-new Mercedes E Class, not the AMG one just the standard E Class, and I pulled up behind him in my Gullwing. He was sorting his bags out when I got out of the car in my chef's jacket, jeans and trainers, carrying my knives. He looked at me and I looked at him. I pulled down the Gullwing door, locked the car, nodded and said, 'All right, mate?' His face. It was brilliant. For that alone it was worth every penny. That and the incredible sound it made every time you put your foot on the accelerator.

I've had faster cars, I've had lighter cars, I've since had more expensive cars, but I've never had a cooler car than the Gullwing. I kind of regret selling it. Then again, I can't complain. I made a small profit when I sold it back to Mercedes to be the centrepiece in their exhibition centre at Brooklands. On the downside, it went up that much again within a year of me selling it to them.

The good news, though, is that this time I put the money to good use. I'd moved from my little converted Baptist church to a house with a reasonable plot of land front and back, and when I sold my biggest asset, the Gullwing, I did the sensible thing with the profits and finally built myself a garage. Well, two six-bay garages actually. So I'd gone from having exceptional cars with nowhere to store them to having exceptional garages and nothing to put in them.

Not that that was a problem for very long.

28 *FOLLOW THAT CAR!*
THE FERRARI 355 AGAIN

I don't know what it is, but sometimes cars just seem to find me. Critically, though, I won't hang about worrying endlessly whether something's right or wrong. I might take time to do some research or have a chat with a mate about it, but I'll know the second I see it. And if it's the right thing, I'm not going to walk away from it just because it's not what I was looking for at that precise moment in time. If it's right, it's right. Simple. If you have to think about it for too long, you're probably best off keeping your wallet in your pocket. And if I've learned anything with all the cars I've bought over the years, it's that the cars that find you are almost always the best buys of all.

The best Ferrari I've ever owned found me one day when I went to put down a deposit on a completely different car. I'd read in a magazine that Ferrari were going to build a new version of the Dino, their classic late sixties/ early seventies roadster. These reported rumours often fail to materialise into anything you can actually drive, but I figured it was worth putting down a deposit. If it did go into production the demand was likely to be phenomenal, and being at the front of the queue was a very exciting and potentially profitable place to be. (As it turned out, the much-rumoured revival of the Dino became just as anticipated as that of their other late sixties roadster, the California, although I'd have to wait another four years to actually see one.)

Pippa and I drove over to the dealer in the Gullwing, which used to make even hardened salesmen drool. It always guaranteed being taken seriously and getting top-flight service too. With the paperwork done and the cheque for the deposit handed over, I turned to walk out – and there, right in front of me, in the middle of the showroom, was a bright red Ferrari 355.

It was a déjà vu experience. I was back in a Ferrari dealership looking at a 355 and getting just as excited as the last time I was looking at one (when, of course, I ended up leaving with a black 360) and the first time back in the Howards' garage. It was exactly the same car. Red, cream leather, F1 paddle gear shift. It was even, to the pound, the same money, at £55,000. It was two models old now – the 355 had been replaced by the 360 and then the 430 – but it still looked fantastic and I suddenly felt an urge to take it out for a test drive. The salesman happily handed the keys over and let me go out for a spin in it by myself. It was one of the best cars I've ever driven. They also had a really nice 550, which is more of a grand tourer, which I also took out for a drive, just because I was curious, and that was great too. But the 355 was the one. It was everything you could want from a performance car. There were no niggles or flaws; they got everything exactly right with it. Just by driving it a couple of hundred yards down the road I knew this was the perfect Ferrari. I'd come so close to buying one before, there was no way I was walking away from it this time. I took it for another quick spin around the block, just to be sure. Not that I needed to, I just wanted to drive it again. When I got back to the showroom I told the salesman I'd take it. Pippa almost fell over. We had, after all, only gone in there to put a deposit down. Driving a new car home really hadn't been part of the plan.

Of course, typically, I didn't actually have the cash with me. But some things are just meant to be. I'd turned round and seen that red 355 there, exactly the same as the one before; it was like someone was trying to tell me something, and I couldn't ignore it. To Pippa and the salesman it no doubt looked like an impulse buy. To me it was an opportunity too good to miss, and I've never for a second regretted grabbing it with both hands (and a little bit of interest free credit). Once again a car found me, and I was very glad it did.

29 *THE TIME OF MY LIFE: THE DBS 007*

The hardest-working person I know, and the most generous, as anyone will agree, is Barbara. I can honestly say that I've never met anyone more committed to their work than Barbara is to film-making and James Bond. She was always, always working. If she wasn't away filming or working on pre- or post-production, she'd be off networking at parties or dinners and charity auctions. (I later found out that the reason she bid so much for me was because she was a proper fan, had all my books and everything. She'd even queued up at the Good Food Show to get them signed, although she always insisted that she just really liked my cooking.)

If there's anyone out there who thinks she got where she is in life just because her dad was a legendary film producer, they're very much mistaken. Not only did she have to work her way up through her dad's company, EON, once she actually took over producing the Bond films with her half-brother Michael, she had the guts to make the changes needed to relaunch Bond, not once, but twice. She's willing to take risks, and they usually pay off. Bringing Pierce Brosnan in completely turned things around and brought Bond back from the dead; then she did it again with Daniel Craig, reinventing everything to make *Casino Royale* the most successful Bond film ever. I remember all the sleepless nights over the script for *Casino Royale*; the idea of taking it all back to the beginning was a huge, huge risk. But she had the balls to do it, and to hire Daniel when everyone was against it. She used to show me letters from film executives who wanted Eddie Murphy to be Bond. Christ, can you imagine? But Barbara believed in Daniel, she believed he was right for the role, and she stuck to her guns. And she was right. Yes, without a doubt Barbara is the hardest-working person I have ever known. You will never meet anyone who deserves everything they get – the success, the money, the lifestyle – more than she does, yet in the four and a half years we were together I never really saw her enjoy it. She certainly never spent anything on herself. Cars (and bikes and boats and watches) have always consumed my money, but she never collected things or had a hobby. She never had time. Don't get me wrong, she loves what she does and she adores her kids. She's had her share of hard times but she's not an unhappy person. I just never saw her indulge herself, that's all. If anything, she drew enjoyment from looking after other people. That's what gave her the most pleasure. She would spare no effort to make someone else happy. Barbara is a very giving person, and when you've got limitless resources, physical and financial, that can mean you're giving a hell of a lot.

The first year we were together, Barbara gave me a Picasso print for my birthday. Yes, a Picasso. We'd gone to an exhibition of work at a London gallery on our first date and there was this one painting that was absolutely stunning. I couldn't stop looking at it. About six months later, Barbara organised a party for my birthday. She'd secretly invited about 40 of my friends without me knowing and they'd shown up with little presents – the usual, key rings, books and that – and then Barbara said, 'Well, I didn't really want to do this here, in front of everyone, but, well, here you are. Happy birthday.' And with that she handed me my present. I unwrapped it, and it was a print of the painting. The Picasso. An absolutely beautiful thing.

Barbara always said that smart money buys art, and that Madonna, who'd just done the theme song for *Die Another Day*, thought the same. Which sounded fair enough, only I wasn't Madonna. I was a chef who now had a Picasso and didn't really know what to do with it. I mean, what do you do with a Picasso? It wasn't something I'd ever given much thought to.

I was doing *Ready Steady Cook* the day after the party. I arrived at the studio in Wandsworth with this artwork in a brown paper bag in the boot of my Audi, because I didn't want to let it out of my sight. But what the hell was I going to do with it? I couldn't leave it in the back of the car, so I kept it locked in my dressing room for six hours while I recorded three shows. Someone suggested it might be an idea to store it at the bank, so I rang Richard, my man at the bank, and asked if he could help me out. He told me to meet him at their branch on The Strand (which incidentally is the most amazing place with big fish tanks full of koi carp) because it had a massive vault.

After finishing *Ready Steady Cook* I drove into central London, parked, and walked down The Strand with the print under my arm in a brown paper bag, praying that nobody decided to mug me. Richard met me at the door, along with a security guard, and led me to the vault. Now, when you're putting something in the vault, they won't take it off you, you have to take it in there yourself and check it in. Richard was filling in all the paperwork and he asked me for the value of the piece, to which I said, 'I don't know.' He gave me a funny look, so I explained that it was a present. Then he asked what the painting was. I told him it was a Picasso. He just laughed.

'No it's not,' he said.

'Yes it is,' I said.

'No it's not,' he insisted. 'People don't just carry Picassos around under their arms in brown paper bags.'

I assured him that this person did, and that there weren't many of these prints around.

While I'm on the subject, there was this time when I tried my own hand at art. I had remembered that Barbara loved a painting she had seen during a visit to Italy, so I looked up the image on the internet and then tried to paint my own version of it to give to her. In the end though, my effort looked more like two whales jumping out of a pond, and definitely nothing like the original. But it was the thought that counted!

Barbara had the most astonishing ability to remember little details. She'd recall that you took one sugar in your tea even if she'd only made you tea once two years ago. If you said you liked a certain restaurant, next birthday you'd be eating there.

We once saw Ronan Keating on *Top of the Pops* and he had this great ring on his little finger which I made an admiring remark about to Barbara. She got me the exact same ring that Christmas. I don't know how she found out what it was or where it came from – she probably called Ronan's management and asked them – but about four weeks later we were sat in my car outside her house, she took out this little Tiffany's box, and when I opened it up I saw it was *that* ring. The thing is, they only made it in girls' sizes (which is why Ronan had it on his little finger), so to get it to fit she'd had it widened with an extra section of diamonds, and while they were at it she'd got them to inscribe it on the inside with our saying: *Being with you is as easy as breathing*. It was exactly the right fit too: apparently she'd checked it on my finger one night while I was asleep. To repay the gesture I had a ring made for her in Winchester, with a few diamonds and the same inscription.

It's hard to buy gifts for the woman who can literally have everything so I always tried to do special things that nobody else could have done.

Barbara always had some unbelievable surprise up her sleeve, the kind of thing money can't buy. I always wanted to go to the French Laundry in the Napa Valley, Thomas Keller's legendary three-star Michelin restaurant; without question it's the greatest in the world. Out of the blue one day Barbara said, 'I've got a surprise for you. We're going on a little trip.' We took a flight from LA to San Francisco, took a car to the Napa Valley, and just walked into the French Laundry. I couldn't believe it. I said something profound like, 'You've got to be joking.' I knew the French Laundry had a year's waiting list for a table, but Barbara had pulled every string there was and personally had a word with people at the highest level. Even after all that she only managed to jump the queue by six months, which tells you how hard this place is to get into. She'd booked it and kept it a secret for six whole months. I don't know who was more excited, her or me.

We walked in through the door, and who was the first person I met? The restaurant manager, who used to be my restaurant manager at the Hotel Du Vin. He looked at me and said, 'All right, chef?'

'All right mate, how ya doing?'

Barbara was standing there looking stunned. 'Do you know each other?' she asked. 'Great. If you only knew the lengths I went to ... and you could have just picked up the phone and got us a table straight away!'

The food was incredible. The best food, the best wine, the best meal I've ever had in my life. It was, quite frankly, unbelievable. I wouldn't let her pay for it though. She'd already done enough organising it all. I couldn't believe that anyone would actually do that for me, so when the bill came I insisted. In total, including wine, that bill came to a fortune. And it was worth every single penny. I can't remember a hell of a lot about what we had as we both got wasted on some phenomenal wine (which mostly explains the bill), but I know it was sensational, and the evening was easily one of the best of my life. That night meant more to me than anything. It was one of my dreams, and she made it happen.

The birthday trip to Italy was the same. Barbara had rented the most beautiful house on the Amalfi coast. She was over there scouting locations or something, she had the kids with her and various other people, and she flew me over for my birthday. I was stood outside one night with Barbara, a couple of days before my birthday, looking out on the breathtaking Amalfi coastline, and I turned to her and said that my mother would absolutely love the place. Unbeknown to me, Mum and Pete were already on a plane over. Barbara had arranged for them to join us. She knew how close I was to my mum and Pete, so she'd always include them. She didn't have to, but she knew it would mean a lot to me, and to them.

When *Casino Royale* was being filmed at Villa D'Este on Lake Como in northern Italy (where Bond's recuperating after getting his balls whacked), I went out, not so much because I wanted to watch the filming but because Villa D'Este holds one of the most famous concours events in the world and I was eager to visit the place. Once a year the rarest and best classic cars converge there, so Villa D'Este is mega famous if you're into cars. We all had a great time, watched all the filming, had a good look around Villa D'Este, which is beautiful, and made the most of the villa we were staying in overlooking the lake. It was great, everything you could ever ask for and more.

Then, when the Bond lot were packing up everything ready to move to the next location, Barbara said to me and Pete, 'Right, you've got a choice. You can come with us to Venice now or you can follow on after you've been to Maranello where I've arranged for you to have a private tour of the Ferrari factory.' Barbara's best mate, Michelle Yeoh, who was a Bond girl in *Tomorrow Never Dies*, was going out with Jean Todt, head of Ferrari. Barbara had put in a call and apparently Jean had arranged the whole thing. Unbelievable. Pete and I were looking at each other, thinking, 'Venice and Bond or Maranello and Ferrari? No contest!'

An early start and a five-hour drive from Lake Como later we pulled up at the Ferrari factory, and 20 minutes after that we were sitting outside Jean Todt's office waiting to see the great man himself. We were soon ushered in, and Jean was there behind his desk. He couldn't speak much English, and my French wasn't really up to deep and meaningful conversation, but we managed to chat for about half an hour about how the F1 season was going and he gave us both some gorgeous signed books. He even apologised for the fact that Michael Schumacher couldn't be there to see us (right in the middle of the driving season). He then told us that he'd organised a tour of the factory, and after that he'd see us for lunch.

If we'd gone home at that moment I know both our lives would have been complete, but as it was Pete and I got the full Maranello tour. First the bits the regular punters saw – the factory museum, the showroom, the shop – then the bits they didn't get to see: the F1 factory where they were putting together Michael Schumacher's race cars; Enzo Ferrari's house in the middle of the Fiorano test track, which is kept like a museum to the Ferrari founder; and finally Schumacher's and Todt's private car collections. You've never seen anything like it: Enzos, FXXs, these were Michael's and Jean's private cars. No one else ever got to see them, and me and Pete were just wandering around, having our pictures taken next to them.

If it hadn't been for our lunch date with Jean we'd probably have stayed in the garages all day looking at those cars. There were so many amazing things to take in, things I'd never seen before (or since). When we got to the restaurant, we walked in and all the Ferrari mechanics were there having their lunch, but our guide wasn't stopping. He led us through the heaving dining room and into a back room. It was like something from *The Godfather*. Sitting at this table at the far end of what turned out to be the private room where Enzo Ferrari used to have his lunch every day was Jean Todt.

Pete and I were sat opposite each other with Jean at the end of the table, and we were all chatting away quite happily about what we'd seen on our tour and about Ferraris and Formula 1 when Jean clocked my watch. He pointed at it and said, 'Nice watch.' I nodded. I'd already seen that he was wearing a fabulous Richard Mille watch, so I said 'Richard Mille?' and he nodded. 'RM10?' I added. I couldn't make out if it was the RM10 or the RM5, so I played it safe and went for the more expensive option. He shook his head and replied, 'No. Richard is a friend of mine. He made this especially for me.'

I felt a little embarrassed, but before I could blush he took it off and handed it to me to have a look at. No exaggeration, this thing weighed no more than an old halfpenny piece. I love my watches, and anyone else who's a fan or a collector will know that these are the business. Jean explained that that was because it was made of magnesium and titanium; what's more, it had a Tourbillon movement, which meant that the watch I was holding couldn't have been worth a penny less than £150,000. I'd never even seen a watch with a Tourbillon movement, never mind held one. I was sitting in the Ferrari factory private dining room having lunch with the boss of Ferrari and holding one of the rarest watches on the planet in my hand. Forget Bond. Watches, Ferraris, Formula 1 – it couldn't get any better than that. And then it did. Before we left, Jean gave me some bottles of Modena balsamic vinegar, because he knew I was a chef as well as a car nut and the two things Modena's famous for are Ferrari and balsamic vinegar. Watches, Ferraris, Formula 1 and food. Now I really was in heaven.

In Venice, we stayed in the Cipriani, which is worth a trip to the city in itself. Filming was quite intense as they had a lot to get through: Daniel Craig and Eva Green sailing into the lagoon on the yacht, the chase through the back streets, the gun fight in the piazza. Later, Pete and I had fun running around the set with prop guns, recreating the explosive piazza scene we'd just seen filmed. The schedule was very, very tight though and everyone was getting stressed out. They only had a couple of days to get all the shots they needed and as usual things were taking longer than they'd thought.

On the last day, while Barbara was otherwise engaged desperately trying to make sure it all got finished, I took my mother shopping to try to find a little present for Barbara. The Maranello trip had been one of the best experiences of my life, something I would never have the chance to do again and something I will never forget, and I wanted to say thank you so very much for it, and for all the other things she'd done for me. I wanted to get her something that made her realise how much all of it had meant to me.

My mother took me to this jeweller's because she recalled that Barbara had liked practically everything they had, and one ring in particular. It was a handmade piece, one of a kind, made of this incredibly fine silver that looked almost like lace. It was beautiful, and I loved it; more importantly, Mum assured me that Barbara loved it, so I told the guy in the shop I'd take it. I didn't ask how much it was, and I couldn't quite see the price tag as he took it off to gift wrap it, but I figured it couldn't be that bad. All right, it was silver, handmade and one of a kind, but it didn't have any diamonds on it so I could probably just about afford it.

I gave the guy my card, and at first, when he punched the numbers in, I thought it was €260,000. To which I understandably thought, 'Fucking hell.' Then I realised that if it was that much the card would be declined anyway so I'd be all right. It was actually €26,000. Not for the first time in my life I found myself trying to do some quick maths in my head. Yes, I should have enough in the account to cover it. It was only when I got home and checked my statement that I realised it had come to something like £17,000 and had completely wiped me out. That was it, all gone. Once again my account was right the way back to zero. Story of my life. I knew I had a pretty major tax bill coming at the end of the next quarter and I was going to be cutting it fine, so I just got my head down and worked my nuts off. I never told anyone that the ring wiped me out. Barbara certainly never knew, and I never told my mother because she'd have gone nuts.

Putting treats to one side for the moment, it's often hard to tell someone how you really feel about them. It's difficult to talk about the big things when you're in a relationship, and if you have a go, you never do it properly. You never say what you meant to say; it just never comes out quite right. For me, it's easier to write things down, especially after the event – and the fact is that Barbara was the first real love of my life. I still think the world of her. I always have and I always will. I'd be there for her tomorrow if anything happened. If there was anything she wanted or needed, I'd be there for her and her kids.

We've both moved on, but it was one of those special

relationships where you never forget the times you had together. She did more for me than anybody else in my life. In fact, she cared so much that I had to be careful what I said. I've had problems with my lower back for years – it's a chef thing, it comes from being hunched over work surfaces all the time. I'd lived with it for years and used to go to an osteopath in Winchester who cracked my back for me – until, that is, Barbara found out. As soon as she heard about it that was it, I was off to the best physio in Harley Street. You learned to keep your gob shut in the end. I also ended up having teeth pulled out by the best dentist in London, and when I said I wanted to get a dog we went to Crufts to find my Clumber Spaniel, Fudge, the one who rearranged that first *Casino Royale* script.

The money itself did not matter to Barbara, it was what it could do for people that was important. That's why nothing was out of the question and there were no lengths she wouldn't go to. There's one story about how once during filming one of the runners' cousins fell quite seriously ill. Barbara had him flown out to the best doctor for treatment. She sorted it. It wasn't a question of cost. She was in a position to do something, so she did. There aren't many people like that.

The days that really stand out for me are the ones when it was just the two of us. We'd switch off our phones – when Barbara's phone was on it'd be absolute mayhem – and it would be our time. But that would only happen four or five times a year, if that. The rest of the time there was such demand for her attention, and it was often hard to compete.

When it was just us we were probably the best couple you could ever put together, proper soul mates, best friends. You could have taken away all the money and all the success and all the houses and all the cars and all the Bond stuff, all of it, and we'd still have been good together, because we clicked. In fact, if you could have taken it all away, we'd probably still be together now. It was everything else that got in the way. Had Barbara and I had nothing it would have made our life together everything. I wanted to be with her and she wanted to be with me; it was all the other stuff that I couldn't handle.

Barbara never put a foot wrong. Everything she did she did with the best of intentions and because she wanted the best for me. That I wasn't happy was down to the fact that I wouldn't change. Because I couldn't change. Not that Barbara ever asked me to, but for the relationship to work I would have had to leave behind everything I understood, the life I'd created for myself, my career, and every principle I'd lived by since as far back as I could remember. And I just couldn't do it.

In our own world, she and I were just a great partnership. In her world, though, I always felt like an onlooker. I felt like I was back outside the Bentley showroom on Berkeley Square, nose pressed up against the glass, knowing that as much as I wanted to be inside I was never going to get there. We would go to dinner parties and people would give me this look that pretty much said, 'Who the hell are you?' I wasn't in the film industry and I didn't know anything about it, which made it hard to move in her circles or ever feel like I had a valid opinion, or indeed a good reason for being wherever it was in the first place. Hollywood, both the place and the industry, is fun to visit, but I wouldn't want to live there. It was so alien, so far removed from everything I knew, and after a while it stopped being fun and exciting. Those parties, the crowded rooms full of people I had nothing in common with, became very lonely places to be. The only other time I'd felt like that was way back when I was working in professional kitchens for the first time, but at least then I always knew that if I worked hard enough I'd be able to compete with everyone else. This time I realised that was never going to happen. I'd worked hard all my life and I'd achieved success in my career, yet I felt like after years of climbing the ladder I'd all of a sudden gone down a long snake right back to the beginning again. I was a British chef, for fuck's sake. If I'd owned 50 restaurants then maybe I'd have been able to move more comfortably in her circles, but as it was there was no way I could compete. Barbara never wanted me to, of course. She would have hated the thought that I felt I needed to compete with her career, her success and her money, but it's hard when you've worked hard all your life and achieved things to be that small fish again.

The age gap didn't help matters either. There was a ten-year difference between us, and when we went to functions I'd feel really uncomfortable when people looked at me, this nobody, and thought, 'He's with her for the money.' They would actually come up to me and say, 'Oh yeah, you're the cook.' That really used to aggravate me. I knew exactly what that meant, and it couldn't have been further from the truth.

But she would always be there by my side to stop people saying things, and now that I look back I can see that it was just me being daft. I sometimes wonder why the hell I cared so much about what they said but, like in any relationship, we can all look back and think, 'Why did I do this, or say that?' You can't change the past so it's something we all have to live with, right or wrong.

With me, work has always come first. As much as I didn't like the hours Barbara used to put into her job, she didn't like the hours I put into mine. It could be an incredibly lonely life when she was away filming. I'd desperately want to be with her, and then when she phoned and said, 'Fly over, I'll send a jet,' I'd usually have *Ready Steady Cook* to do, or a demo in Hull, or something else. It was hard to meet in the middle. On the one hand I know she respected what I did and my commitment to my work: I missed the *Die Another Day* royal premiere because I was doing a pan demo in Debenhams on Oxford Street. This was one of the many things that get booked into my diary up to a year in advance, and I think it's important not to let people down and to honour your commitments. It was funny though – I was stood there cooking pork chops in my new non-stick frying pan, in front of six grannies and a baby, and all the while I was getting text messages from Barbara telling me that things were going brilliantly and that she'd see me at the after-show party. Straight after the demo I drove to Hyde Park and to the party. But parking was such a nightmare that I ended up putting the car outside One Ninety

Queen's Gate and changing into my dinner jacket in the back seat.

My dedication to work meant there were often crazy days like that. And when I said to Barbara that I hated us always being apart, she said, 'Why don't you give it all up, then? I'll look after you.' Well, that was the last thing I wanted. To be given a cheque every week? No thanks. I could have just jetted around the world with Barbara, staying in all the best hotels, eating in all the best restaurants. The thing is, I wanted to work. Obviously there was no way Barbara was going to walk away from her life; there was no way she could, and I wouldn't have asked her to. So I suppose the stalemate we ended up with was inevitable.

It was that day we went with Daniel Craig to Aston Martin's HQ to see the clay model of the car for *Casino Royale* that it really hit home just how far apart our worlds were and how impossible it was going to be to find a middle ground. More specifically, when we all started talking about what colour the car should be. After I'd picked the right kind of silver, I'd added, 'Of course, if it was for me personally, I'd go for black on black – black paint, black interior.'

Barbara said, 'Well have one if you want one.'

I laughed. 'No, it's all right.'

She was insistent. 'Have one.' She was genuinely going to write a cheque right there and then and buy one. This was the brand-new Aston Martin DBS, and she was just going to write a cheque for it.

I told her not to be so ridiculous, but she was already

talking to Ulrich Betz, the head of Aston Martin, saying, 'Yes, we'll have it black, with black interior, and we'll have the chassis number 007,' and Ulrich was saying, 'Yeah, yeah, yeah, great, fine, no problem,' and I was saying, 'No we won't.'

I really don't think Barbara got what my problem was because she just kept saying, 'Why not? If you want it we'll get it.' I tried to explain to her that it was excessive, that you can't just give someone a car as a gift. A watch is a gift. A ring is a gift. A bracelet is a gift. A car is too much. It's not like it was even my birthday or Christmas; it was just a spur-of-the-moment thought. In the end I said to her, 'If I want something, I'll work for it. Just drop it or we're going to fall out over this.' But she and Ulrich continued to organise it so I just left them to it. I don't know what happened in the end. She probably bought it. She's probably got a black on black Aston Martin DBS, chassis number 007, in a garage somewhere.

I could see where she was coming from. She wanted to do it because she thought it would make me happy, and all she ever wanted to do was make me happy. But there was no way I could accept it. It's one of the principles I got from my dad: you work for everything, and what you deserve is what you work for. If you wanted a Mini and you earned the money for a Mini and you bought a Mini, then that's success. Success isn't financial, success is all about achievement. The biggest success in my life came when I was 21, the day I was appointed a head chef. My achievements are reflected in the house I live in and the cars in my garage.

When I get up of a morning and open the doors of my garages and see the cars inside, I'm still amazed by what I've achieved. The way I see it, if somebody just comes along, says there you go and gives it to you, it's not the same. If I'd let Barbara buy that car I'd always have looked at it and thought, 'I don't deserve that. What have I done to deserve that? Nothing.' I've worked for everything all my life. Since being packed off to London on a train with a £50 note in my pocket, everything I now have I've worked for. That was all going to change if I let someone just write a cheque and put a mega money car in my garage. And it would have ticked all the boxes for all those people who said I was only with her for the money. If I was given expensive cars, how the hell was I going to walk into a room, hold my head up and face these people?

It was a pretty defining moment in our relationship. Deep down I knew there was always going to be an imbalance. The money, the power, the hours, the time apart, the priorities, all of these things were going to be issues we would never resolve. For that to happen I'd have had to change completely, and I couldn't do it. In my head, I didn't want to spend the rest of my life like that, much as my heart was saying otherwise.

Barbara wanted to be with me. I know that. It was me who couldn't cope with the relationship. I remember having a long conversation with my mum, saying to her that I didn't think I could handle it any more. 'You're mad,' she said. 'You've got a woman there who adores you, who you absolutely adore. Forget about all the other stuff, that's irrelevant, it's just the two of you.' But only rarely was it just the two of us. There was a whole other life there I never felt part of.

To walk away from someone you love and who loves you that much, someone who would do absolutely anything for you, is hard, and maybe it was the daftest thing I've ever done in my life, but it was probably the most sensible thing I've ever done too. In the end I think it was for the best, not just for Barbara and me but for her kids as well. I think they all needed somebody a bit older who was in the same industry, or at least knew a bit about it, someone who could be more a part of their world.

A couple of years later, after *Casino Royale* had come out and been a huge success and the Aston Martin DBS had finally gone into production and was on sale to the public, I test-drove it for my motoring column in the *Mail on Sunday*'s *Live* magazine. It looked exactly the same as that clay model, only it was in the same silver as Daniel's in the film, the colour I'd picked for it. What was it like? Magic. Absolutely magic. Every bit as fun and exciting as the clay model had promised it would be. Easily one of the best cars I've tested for the magazine, one of the best cars I've ever driven full stop. I'd definitely have one. Or at least I would if I had a spare £170,000.

30 *STRICTLY KNACKERED*

There are two things in this world I know a lot about, and dancing isn't one of them. If it's cars or cooking, I'm sorted. I can talk about Maseratis, Mustangs and Mercedes all day long, and if it's a 2,000-calorie portion of white chocolate and whisky bread and butter pudding you're after, I'm your man. But the only salsa I like comes with Doritos, and my cha-cha isn't a pretty sight. I am not a natural mover, unless it involves wheels. I picked cookery over PE at school, for God's sake; that should tell you all you need to know about my athletic abilities. My agent Fiona and my PA Pippa decided to ignore this evidence, however, and ganged up on me by accepting the BBC's kind invitation for me to be a contestant on *Strictly Come Dancing*. They also conveniently chose to forget that I hate reality TV with a passion only matched by my dislike of modern American cars and Volvos. And that's saying something.

I was away on *Ocean Village* when Fiona got the call. She spoke to Pippa and between them they decided it was a good idea and that was it, I was doing it. Fiona knew better than to ask me. She knew what my answer would be, and just how colourfully I'd put it too. The first I heard of it was when I got back from the trip, by which time it was too late to pull out as rehearsals started in two weeks.

Of course I've long since forgiven Fiona and Pippa for neglecting to ask my opinion. If they had, I'd have said no without even thinking about it, and then I'd have missed out not just on one of the most intense, challenging and rewarding experiences of my life, but also on the chance to raise my profile and open doors to opportunities that might otherwise never have come my way. Would I have got my first prime-time BBC series *Sweet Baby James* or been asked to take over *Saturday Kitchen* when Antony Worrall Thompson left if it hadn't been for *Strictly*? Who knows, but it certainly didn't hurt. So I'm pleased they put me up for it. At the time, however, I was anything but pleased. If I remember rightly, I swore quite a lot.

To be honest, though, after the initial shock of finding out that I had to do it, I resigned myself to the fact that I'd probably only be in it for a week or two anyway, so maybe it wasn't such a big deal after all. When I got there for the first night of the live show, I looked around the green room and saw all these famous faces. Everybody else was talking to one another and I was like Billy-no-mates, in the corner. Gloria Hunniford was there, Zoe Ball, Patsy Palmer, Colin Jackson, Darren Gough, all people I'd heard of. Who'd heard of me? I was a chef on *Ready Steady Cook*. Once again I was back to being a small fish in a big pond. I'd been booked out of the diary for six weeks, but now I was convinced this would be my one and only appearance.

From beginning to end, I was on the show for twelve weeks. I threw everything I had at it. I decided that if I was going to do it I was going to give it 100 per cent, like I do with all my work. I wanted to get it right, and not just for myself. My dance partner, Camilla Dallerup, was a world-class professional and extremely competitive. She was there to win and I didn't want to let her down and make her look bad, so I worked my arse off to get it absolutely bang-on. Even Camilla was knackered at the end of it.

That first night, though, I was absolutely terrified. I just suddenly realised how out of my depth I was. I don't think I could get further out of my comfort zone if I tried. I was sitting there in the dressing room, petrified, when Fiona knocked on the door. She came in, sat down, looked me in the eye and said, 'This is it. This is your chance. I can't do any more for you now, it's up to you. The door's open, don't waste it.' Every night when I went out there I had those words in my mind, and every night I tried my absolute best.

I couldn't believe it when I didn't get sent home that first night. I genuinely thought I'd be out in the first round. Then I got through again, and again. Suddenly we were halfway through the competition and Camilla began to say to me, 'You can do this, you can go all the way, you can do it.' The problem was, as it got nearer to Christmas my work commitments were increasing and it was getting harder and harder to keep all the plates spinning. I did the Good Food

Show right in the middle of the series, and that was the first real indication I got of just what a big deal *Strictly* was. I really hadn't believed it would make much of a difference to my profile until I walked out as part of the *Ready Steady Cook* team and got a bigger cheer than Ainsley Harriott and Antony Worrall Thompson put together. That's when I started to think that things might be about to change. I somehow managed to screw up every single dish during that demo and I still trounced Antony. It was surreal. Then, having done nine till six at the Good Food Show, I'd have an hour off and then be training with Camilla in some work-shop in Birmingham until two in the morning. At the same time I was filming *Castle in the Country* with John Craven for the BBC, so Camilla and I would practise during my lunch break. Literally, wherever I was working, Camilla and the film crew would be there. They followed me absolutely everywhere because it was the only way we could get the practice in.

I don't think I've ever worked so hard. Between cheffing, TV work and *Strictly*, I was grafting harder than I did when I was at One Ninety Queen's Gate, and I hadn't thought that was possible. I lost 3 stone in six weeks. I was quite pleased about that, but the combination of the physical exercise of the dancing and working unbelievable hours began to take their toll.

On top of it all, the newspapers, egged on by the BBC's press machine, had decided that Camilla and I were more than just dance partners and were running daily updates on our supposed romance. That might sound harmless enough, but at the time I was still with Barbara, who was having to read every day about this great love affair I was apparently having before, during and after rehearsals, and Camilla's boyfriend was having to do the same. And while the tabloids making up facts isn't particularly news to anyone, when BBC2's *Strictly* spin-off programme *It Takes Two* framed Camilla and me in a big pink love heart when we went on, it was too much. We ended up rehearsing in secret to avoid being followed everywhere by photographers, and when that didn't work we decided to do an interview with the *Mirror*. We did it in a dance studio in Richmond, and the next day they printed a four-page spread with the headline 'James Martin and Camilla in Love'. There wasn't a single word in the piece that supported the headline, but they had a picture of me and Camilla on the cover next to a picture of Jude Law and Sienna Miller as the two hot celebrity couples of the moment. By this point we were both working ridiculously hard, we were exhausted, and our relationships were starting to feel the strain.

The moment it hit home just how well we were doing on the show was when we knocked Patsy Palmer out to make it through to the semi-finals. We were bottom two for the second week in a row, it was down to the public vote, and I was up against Bianca from *EastEnders*. I thought there was no way I'd survive. As we were waiting for the result I turned to Camilla and said, 'That's it, we're off, we're going.' She was saying, 'No, you're not, you're staying, you're staying.' And we did. I couldn't believe it. I was a bloke off *Ready Steady Cook* and she was Bianca on a popular prime-time soap. She was mega famous. How did that happen? It was amazing, such a high.

But I'd had it. I was knackered, I was fed up, I was resenting all the stories in the papers, I hadn't seen Barbara in weeks, and I'd just had enough. I just couldn't do it any more. Before we did the live semi-final show on the Saturday night we had to pick our music so that the orchestra had time to rehearse it. We were given a list of tracks to pick from and I chose Michael Bublé's 'Home', the one with the line 'I wanna go home' in it. And I really did. Sure enough, the next week we went out. I know I couldn't have given it any more. I did my absolute best, and I was proud that we'd got so far.

It remains one of the best things I've done, and one of the hardest. I loved all the ballroom dances, but I hated the Latin. The ballroom suited my height. The Latin I was more than happy to leave to Colin Jackson; he always had a thing for spandex and sequins. I did actually buy a couple of my outfits, including my ballroom gear, which I ended up wearing by mistake to a black-tie dinner after I grabbed the wrong suit out of the wardrobe. It was a charity do at a hotel miles away so I couldn't even go back home to get my proper DJ. I had to spend a very uncomfortable evening in trousers that weren't designed for sitting down and a jacket in which putting your arms down by your side was almost a physical impossibility. That I bought the outfits proves that I enjoyed the *Strictly* experience, despite all the hard work and heartache that went with it.

Work-wise I had no complaints either. The series

finished at the end of December and by the new year the phone was ringing off the hook. I was getting bookings for gigs left, right and centre. Richard and Judy wanted me to do a series of one-off cooking segments on their teatime show, which turned into a regular slot. But it wasn't until the Good Food Show came around again in November that I knew for certain I'd entered a different league entirely. Before *Strictly*, as part of the *Ready Steady Cook* show I was doing demos on the Bacofoil stand to a hundred people; the year after *Strictly* I did two shows on my own in front of about four thousand in a purpose-built theatre. After 16 years of slogging my guts out over a hot stove, three months of foxtrotting on BBC1 had finally secured me a seat with the big boys. Looked like Pippa and Fiona were right after all.

31 *MISS ENGLAND AND THE SATURDAY KITCHEN CARS*

My chef Chris and I were in the bar on *Ocean Village*. We were both exhausted after a hell of a night's service. We must have done more than 200 covers. My bistro's always busy, but when I'm there it goes ape shit. Word spreads through the ship like wildfire that you're on board and cooking in the kitchen and suddenly everybody wants a table. And if I'm on board, I am in the kitchen from the first table to the last, and I don't go out into the restaurant until it's all done. I've always felt it's important to be there through everything with the other guys. I'm not there to get a sun tan and wander round like the big 'I am', I'm there to work.

It was about one in the morning. Chris and I were just chilling in the bar, having a beer – or a gin and tonic in Chris's case – when these four models walked in, two guys and two girls. They were shooting a new brochure for *Ocean Village* and they'd just finished for the day. I noticed Sally the instant she walked in because she had this green dress on and she was absolutely stunning. I nudged Chris and said, 'She's all right. A bit out of my league, but you can look, can't you?' With that, Chris and I went back to our drinks and a discussion about what we were going to do with the red mullet for tomorrow.

Next thing, the four of them had clocked me and Chris sitting on our own and come over to join us. We got chatting, Sally asked what we were doing on board and I told her we'd just finished in the restaurant. After chatting for a while, I mentioned I'd been asked to run the London marathon and Chris started taking the piss. We joked about chaffing and Sally said, 'I'll rub your vaseline in if you want.' That's how I met Sally Kettle, Miss England 2001.

Now, I've met more than my share of beautiful and talented women in my time. I've been very lucky. But Sally's special. Sally's not like the rest. It's not because she was Miss England 2001 and danced with Nelson Mandela at the Miss World finals in South Africa. It's not because she's a gifted photographer who's as brilliant behind the camera as she is beautiful in front of it. And it's not even because she's a superstar DJ (especially if you like a bit of pop) who's gigged all over the world for Vodafone. No, the reason Sally's special, the thing that sets her apart from all the other women I've known and which makes her the perfect woman, is this: Sally likes cars. She *really* likes cars. Beauty, brains, a good laugh and a love of driving fast in cool cars. Really, a man cannot ask for more. Her cooking isn't bad either.

Everything was pretty crazy when Sally and I first got together. Work was hectic and my stress levels weren't being helped by the *Saturday Kitchen* phone-in furore. *Saturday Kitchen* was by far the biggest thing to happen to me. My old boss Antony Worrall Thompson had presented it for years, and when he went off to ITV, taking everything but the name with him, the BBC were going nuts. Being asked to replace him and front an all-new *Saturday Kitchen* was a big deal, and accepting the challenge was a big risk. I would be going up not just against my old boss but the host who'd made the format successful. In order to do *Saturday Kitchen* I also had to give up *Ready Steady Cook*, the show that had put a roof over my head and cars in my garage for most of my career. If it worked, I was made. If it failed, my TV career and any primetime aspirations I had would be over. It was a massive gamble for me, but it paid off big style. On our very first week we had an incredible 1.2 million viewers, which was over twice as many as *Saturday Cooks* got over on ITV (they got 500,000). The previous incarnation of *Saturday Kitchen* had averaged 600,000 viewers, so we had instantly doubled the audience. By the end of the year we had nearly three times ITV's viewing figures. They then dropped to 300,000, and eventually threw in the towel and moved to a different time slot. By February 2007 we were getting 2 million viewers, about a third of all people watching television on a Saturday morning. (We still win the slot every week, and *Saturday Cooks* is off the air.)

Then, suddenly, everything seemed to fall apart. The press were looking for any programme doing phone-ins, and they found *Saturday Kitchen*. At the time I was also filming *Sweet Baby James*, which meant we needed to pre-record a handful of *Saturday Kitchen*s in order to fit everything in. To my mind it was all innocent enough. The programmes were recorded as live and two endings were filmed, one featuring the celebrity guest's chosen 'food heaven', the other with their 'food hell'. When the programme aired, viewers phoned in as usual to cast their votes; they were tallied, and the appropriate taped footage was shown. That was television. That's how it was made and always had been. Those handful of shows may not actually have been live, but the net result was the same and the Beeb certainly never made any money doing those type of phone-ins. The papers tried to make out that we were cheating the viewers in some way by 'pretending' it was live when it was a pre-record. This was rubbish; our viewers didn't care because they got to vote in the same way and their votes counted.

What really hurt was that I felt like I was being blamed for something. The papers were looking for famous faces to front stories, and before I knew what was happening, I had photographers on ladders trying to take pictures over my hedge at home, and reporters with megaphones shouting that there were serious allegations and I needed to come out and answer them. All I knew was *Saturday Kitchen* was everything I'd worked for and that it meant everything to me. I was convinced the BBC were going to take it off air and never put it back on again. It's easy to look back now and see it for the passing tabloid storm that it was, but at the time it really did feel like my world was in freefall and I couldn't do anything about it.

Feeling harassed and certain that the end of my TV career was imminent, I needed to get away, if only for a couple of days. I had a flick through the *AA Guide* with Sally, we found a hotel in Kent that looked all right, packed a few bits and pieces, and the next day, after *Saturday Kitchen*, headed straight off. The following morning I was meant to be doing a photo shoot for a magazine, but I just thought, 'I can't go to work today.' For the first time in my entire career and life, I threw a sickie. The one and only time. I simply phoned Fiona and said, 'I'm not working today, tell them I can't make it.' Fiona thought something terrible had happened because I'd never cancelled anything. When Pippa heard she called me and asked if I was all right. I said I was fine but I didn't say what I was doing. No one knew about Sally then. I hadn't even told my mum.

With the whole day in front of us, I said to Sal, 'Let's go somewhere else, let's go to Brighton.'

'Great,' Sal said. 'Can I drive?'

I still had the red 355 then and Sally had never driven a Ferrari and was absolutely desperate to, so I said she could drive it to the end of the hotel drive, which was about half a mile long. Sixty-eight miles and two hours later we arrived in Brighton with Sally still at the wheel. I couldn't get her out of the damn thing. She loved it. That's when I knew she was the girl for me.

That afternoon we just bummed about, and I've never felt so comfortable. We weren't going to a big dinner, or a flash restaurant, or some celebrity-filled party. I've never really been into all that stuff anyway. We just sat on the beach at Brighton and had fish and chips and an ice cream with a Flake. The sun was shining and it was great. At that moment life changed for me. Up til then I'd been living in a bubble, but suddenly I felt at home again. It felt so right to be with Sally. For the first time I felt like I was in a normal relationship, and I'd not had one of those for so long. My relationships to that point had been surreal experiences, amazing but surreal, conducted at 100 miles an hour, all over the place, never enough room for the simple things like just being together, bumming around, doing nothing other than sitting on a beach and eating fish and chips and a 99 with a Flake. Being with Sally chilled me out, and I needed chilling out. I was a stressed bloody nightmare. With Sally I didn't have to prove anything or try to be someone I wasn't. She just made me feel normal, which I hadn't felt for the past ten years.

Less normal is her willingness to share my passion for motors. Some might say she hasn't really got a lot of choice, but then again, how many other girls could you buy a quad bike for as a birthday gift and not end up single by the end of the evening? The first year we were together I was at a loss for what to get her. I've never really been into buying her expensive jewellery or designer clothes. And, to be frank, when Sally gets her hands on my card, it's not Prada she heads for, it's Primark. And she looks bloody great in it too. (Although one thing all men should know, however, is that every girl needs great shoes.) I remembered that she'd said she liked my Harleys and wanted to learn to ride, so one day I was flicking through a car magazine and saw an advert for the Yamaha Raptor, a serious road quad. Thinking that four wheels were a safer place to start than two, I got it for her. She loved it. She was chuffed to bits, couldn't wait to get out on it. First time she went out on it, though, I got a panicked phone call from her. 'I'm in a field, I'm stuck,' she told me. 'Can you come and help me?' When you live in the country, 'I'm in a field' doesn't really narrow it down much. I drove around for about an hour, and eventually found her. She'd come up against a gate she couldn't get through, but she was too close to it to be able to turn. She needed to reverse, but she didn't know how to. I flicked the switch, the one with the big 'R' on it, she reversed, shouted her thanks and just drove off and left me there. Women, eh?

I'm not saying Sally's approved of everything I've bought. A few of my purchases she's disapproved of quite vocally, at least until she drove them. In particular she took an instant dislike to the Lotus 340R I bought one week after *Saturday Kitchen*. To be honest, I'm not surprised she didn't like the look of it. It's a totally mad toy, completely impractical, but nothing goes round a roundabout quite like it. It's literally just four wheels, two seats and an engine. No doors, no roof, nothing. It's a cheap, fun car to drive. I'd had one before, sold it, and decided I shouldn't have, so I phoned the guy who'd bought it to see if he fancied selling it back to me. He told me that he'd just that week totalled it, driven it into a ditch.

Of course, as soon as I knew I couldn't have that one, I wanted one even more and I went out on a mission. I found one in a dealership in Kent, got Sally to pick me up from the studio after *Saturday Kitchen*, drove straight down there and bought it.

'Don't you want to take it for a test drive?' the dealer asked.

'No need,' I told him. 'I'll take it.'

Sal thought it was a waste of money, and why wasn't I test-driving it? She thought the whole thing was stupid.

A few months later she was getting ready to go shopping, reminding me that I still hadn't taken the Lotus out since it had been delivered and what a waste of money it had been. So I told her to take the Lotus to the shops. Pippa was there and was laughing because she'd once driven my old one to run an errand and we didn't see her for five hours she had such a good time. It's a nuts car. Three hours later, Sally returned from the shops practically bouncing off the walls, telling me what an amazing car it was and how I was never allowed to sell it. I think her exact words were 'You're not selling that fucking thing'.

Yep, on the whole, Sally's been very understanding when it comes to my car obsession, which is just as well, because from the moment I started doing *Saturday Kitchen* this obsession, along with my collection, went into overdrive. *Saturday Kitchen* is lethal for me because I get to drive past loads of showrooms and dealerships on my way to and from the studio, and there's a lot of waiting around during rehearsals when there's nothing else to do but read car magazines. I've bought two motorbikes, a Harley and a Ducati, and a moped, which I rode all the way back home from London to Winchester. (I'll never do that again, it took me bloody ages.) Then there's the 340R, my beautiful mint condition baby blue '59 Corvette (the one Autoglym used to use on their stands at motor shows), and a fully working Jordan F1 racing car. I got Eddie Jordan to sign its nose when we had him on the show a couple of weeks later.

If there's one *Saturday Kitchen* car that Sally's really attached to, it's her 'Little Beenie'. There was a classic car auction I wanted to go to at the NEC in Birmingham, but it was on a Saturday and it started at one pm. I was trying to work out how I was going to get from *Saturday Kitchen*, which finishes at 11:30 am, all the way up to Birmingham in time for the start. I'd been given a good cheque the week before so I thought, 'Sod it, we'll get a helicopter.' But I didn't tell Sally. I told her to meet me at Battersea train station at 11.45 and I'd pick her up in the car. She thought it was a bit odd that I wanted to meet in Battersea; there's not much there other than the old power station and the heliport. We pulled up at the heliport, the helicopter was waiting for us, and it whizzed us straight up to the NEC. We landed, ran across the car park and made it just in time for the lot I wanted, a Porsche 911 RS Touring. It went for £150,000, £40,000 more than my limit. I was disappointed because I really liked it, and it was a bit of an anticlimax after all the excitement of flying up in the helicopter.

I flicked through the catalogue, and three lots away was a little Fiat 500 Abarth. As you know, I love those little old 500s, and this one was a proper Abarth racing one, listed with an estimate of £20,000 to £22,000. I pointed it out in the catalogue to Sal and she instantly fell in love with it. We quickly went to give it the once-over. It all looked good, then as it came up Sal grabbed the bidding card out of my hand and said, 'Can I?' Instead of subtly raising our number she was there waving it in the air, practically shouting 'More, more!' But we did all right: when the hammer went down the price was just £8,200.

From then on, the little Fiat Abarth was classed as Sally's car because she'd bid for it. I paid for it, but I was left under no illusions. 'Little Beenie', as she called it, was her car. She'd never had a classic car in her life though, so when we got it back we went through it with a fine-tooth comb to work out what was what. We were looking at the fuel pump and there was something not quite right with it. We took it off and removed the fuel line, which should be quite flexible. We bent it and it snapped. I looked at it and it said 'SodaStream. For Food Use Only' on it. If that had snapped while someone was driving it would have sprayed fuel all over the engine and the whole thing would have gone up in flames. The fuel pump itself was mounted on a thin piece of metal that could be bent as easy as anything; on closer inspection it turned out to be a 7Up can that some mad Italian mechanic had flattened and drilled a couple of holes in.

After that we took the whole thing apart to make sure

there weren't any more nasty surprises. Thankfully, everything else was fine, so we put it back together. Sally was almost bouncing off the walls she was so excited by the thought of getting in and driving it. When she eventually pulled out of the drive, turned left and pottered off up the road, she had a big grin on her face; she couldn't have been happier.

About three minutes later I got a phone call.

'Er, I've broken down,' Sally said.

The throttle cable had snapped. I went to get her and tow the car back and found her at the side of the road, standing next to her broken-down Beenie, looking all sad and pitiful. We tied the stricken 500 to the back of my car, and I gave her a hug.

'Welcome to the world of classic cars, Sal.'

32 CAMPERVANS

That's *campervans*, not caravans. There's a difference. A big one. A caravan is something you pull, slowly, behind your Volvo estate, stopping off every couple of miles to have tea from a thermos on the hard shoulder. A campervan, technically speaking, is a self-propelled vehicle that provides both transport and sleeping accommodation. My campervan is like a whole house on wheels. A big house on wheels. It's the biggest thing you can drive without needing an HGV licence. And don't even start imagining a lime-green VW Campervan here either. I'm not Jamie Oliver. We're talking state of the art: fully air conditioned, GPS navigated, satellite dish on the roof, LCD TV, full kitchen, shower, king-size double bed, parking sensors, reversing cameras, the lot. It's the kind of thing racing drivers and rock stars take on the road with them – and I should know: mine was previously owned by F1 champion Nigel Mansell, and it was a rock star who got me into them in the first place.

I don't do 'celebrity' friends. I prefer real ones. The fact that me and Jamiroquai singer Jay Kay get on so well has nothing to do with the fact that we've both had run-ins with the tabloids and everything to do with the fact that he's as mad about cars as I am. The only difference is, he's got a bigger budget. He also grows his own veg and wants to learn how to cook, so we've got plenty to talk about. Most of the time, though, we talk about cars. If I had a pound for every minute we've spent on the phone talking about this car that's coming out or that car we've both spotted on eBay I'd have enough to buy a Ferrari Enzo, just like Jay's. One day. If we're playing real-life Top Trumps, though – which is a bad idea as Jay will always beat me – the one category I'd definitely win is campervans, which is funny because I'd never even thought about getting one until I saw his.

The first time I actually went over to his place – yes, you've heard it before, but it's the only way I can adequately describe it – I was like a kid in a sweet shop. I had a good look round his garages, checking out his collection, making mental notes of things to add to my wish list. For lunch we went out on his lake, caught a couple of trout, cooked them with some veg from the garden, and then, as we were wandering back to the garages, I spotted this motorhome. I pointed at it, laughed and said something along the lines of 'What the hell do you want that for?' Jay replied that I could take the piss all I liked but it was the best thing you could buy. He told me I'd have more fun in a campervan than I would in any car. I was thinking, 'What the hell's he talking about? He's got all these incredible cars. How can a campervan possibly be more fun?' I wasn't at all convinced, but as he gave me a guided tour of this campervan – the shower, the fridge, the motorbike on the back – he was getting more excited about it than any of the cars we'd been looking at earlier.

He must have seen that I was secretly quite taken with it because he started saying that I should get one because I was away a lot with work. It's more comfortable than a hotel, more convenient, in the long term it'll be cheaper ... he used all the magic words you need to hear to convince yourself that the new toy you now want is actually an essential tool you really can't live without. And it worked. All the way home I was thinking that, actually, I really could use one. I *was* away a lot with work, I *was* always in hotels, I *was* always getting hire cars to cart all my gear about, this *would* be easier, cheaper and more convenient, and it might even be quite good fun. Then there were the track days. I could use it for when I took my F1 car out. Suddenly it all made perfect sense. Obviously I didn't tell anyone what I was thinking, least of all Sally. I knew she'd go nuts at the idea.

A couple of days later I had an afternoon off so I decided to go down to this place in Portsmouth that specialised in motorhomes, see what they had and what they cost. I had a budget of about £50,000 in mind because Jay had said that should get me a good one. He'd also given me a couple of tips on what to look out for: forget the bedroom and the kitchen, the first thing to do was stand in the shower, because it didn't matter how good the rest of it was, if the shower was too small it would drive you mad. The vehicles this place had went from a £9,000 trailer my dog wouldn't have been happy sleeping in to a £200,000 palace on wheels, with twin showers, dressing room, 50 inch TV, the full works. Luckily you needed an HGV licence to drive it, so I couldn't have that. I took a load of brochures with me but there wasn't really anything that I liked.

The following week I was testing a Subaru for the *Mail on Sunday*. I couldn't think of anything to write about it, so I thought I'd try to tie it in with motorhomes somehow, try to make it a bit more interesting. I phoned my editor, who loved the idea. He said he'd organise a press pass for the Motorhome and Caravan Club exhibition at the NEC.

When I arrived, the disabled and VIP car parks were one and the same, which should have been the first clue. I was in a souped-up Subaru with blacked-out windows and big fat exhaust pipes and I was parking next to all these Volvos and cars with disabled badges. I looked round to my right and there was an old boy in the passenger seat of the car next to me I was sure was dead until his wife gave him his oxygen mask, which perked him up a bit. As I walked up to the main entrance I saw that half the attendees had walking frames. It was like a mass exodus to the last bingo hall on earth. It didn't really feel like a comfortable place to be. It's fine when Jay Kay is there telling you how great camper-vans are; it takes on a different slant when you meet the rest of the campervan community and half of them are on oxygen. I was wearing a cap and dark glasses, and I had my collar up. I was going in incognito.

No sooner had I walked through the door than one of the event staff pointed at me and said, 'James Martin, what are you doing here?' I was asking myself the very same question. I explained that I was there to do a piece for the *Mail* and she went off and sorted out my credentials.

Once I was in the hall I thought I'd have a really quick scoot round and then get off. Forget the caravans, not interested in those; I went straight for the motorhomes. Literally every single stand I went to I was recognised straight away by the salesmen, all of whom looked at me like I was nuts and invariably asked what on earth I wanted one of these for. Each time I tried to play it cool, saying I wanted it for track days, for when I was racing my F1 car and doing a few classic car historic races and other bits and pieces.

I had a quick look round these motorhomes, and most of them were terrible. Either the shower was too small or there was no room to cook anything. Then I went and had a look at some of the American ones, which were really good value, but like American cars, the build quality wasn't there. Every time you touched something it came off in your hand. Everything was plastic. Then I got chatting to a salesman from the company I'd been to see in Portsmouth. He told me they had a really good one coming in soon that they were taking in part exchange. It was about a year old and had been owned by an ex-Formula 1 driver. Could be exactly what I was looking for, I should come down and have a look at it.

I went down there a week or so later and within about 15 minutes of seeing it I'd bought it. Ten thousand miles on the clock, just a year old, Nigel Mansell part-exchanged it for a bigger one. I'd hate to try and get the one he part-exchanged it for round a tight corner. This one was big enough. It was bigger than Jay's.

As soon as I got it, the first person I called to tell was Jay. He thought it was great. He just kept saying, 'Mate, you'll love it, you'll absolutely love it.' The rest of my mates weren't so convinced. Most of them thought I was an idiot for buying it. Sally wasn't best pleased either. 'What do you want that for? It's stupid.' I think those were her exact words. Still, once she'd had her way with it – filled it with candles and cushions and made it all girly – she liked it a bit more; after we went away in it the first time, she loved it.

Because we'd had such a good time in Brighton the first time we went down there, and we hadn't had a chance to go back since, we loaded up the fridge, booked a campsite and off we went. I've since learned that there's a lot of demand for spaces in campsites, and if you want a good pitch in a decent area you really need to book well in advance. The site we pulled into was a bit more on the pony-and-trap end of the campsite scale. But it didn't matter. We locked the windows and the doors and had a great time. Sally was cooking, I was watching Sky TV in the bedroom, and she just started dancing around saying, 'I love it, I love it.' After that she was pretty much sold. We woke up in the morning, had a hot shower, cooked some breakfast, got the motorbikes out and rode into Brighton. We had fish and chips and an ice cream, as we had a year earlier, had a go on the grabber games (I won a teddy bear for Sally after putting about £60 in the thing), and it was fantastic.

About two months after I took delivery of my house on wheels I got a call from Jay. It was a Friday afternoon and he was at Goodwood for the Festival of Speed. Was I coming? I said I'd love to but I had *Saturday Kitchen* to do the next day. Not a problem, he said, he'd save me a pitch next to his.

When I finished *Saturday Kitchen*, I hoofed it home on one of my motorbikes, got changed, loaded the camper up with provisions, and Sally and I headed off to Goodwood. When we got there, Jay, true to his word, had actually pegged out a pitch for my van. I reversed in, Jay guiding me – 'To me, to me' – the satellite dish went up, the chairs came out, the beers were opened, and we just sat there killing ourselves laughing.

There were loads of other people there with campervans, but none like ours. Ours are proper ones. Ours aren't the kind of campers you find at the Motorhome and Caravan Club exhibition. They're state-of-the-art motorhomes. There's a difference, and it's a big one.

33 *A LEAP OF FAITH: THE MASERATI A6GCS*

You can't just go and stick any old motor in the Mille Miglia. The rules on eligibility are very specific, and the organisers apply them very strictly. The exact wording of the official Registration Regulation for Eligible Cars is as follows:

> 'Cars permitted to take part in the event will be vehicles that have competed, or completed registration, in at least one of the original Mille Miglia races (1927–1957), as well as other exemplars of the same make and model.'
>
> www.1000miglia.eu

The car manufacturers that made the kind of cars that were entered into the original Mille Miglia races were producing only a handful of cars at the time. Ferrari may well have been turning out three hundred cars a year by the sixties, but in the forties and fifties they weren't making it into double digits.

Which of course means that Mille Miglia-eligible cars are both rare and terrifyingly expensive. Million-plus budgets aren't uncommon, and most people will spend a year or more getting their car ready for the race. When the BBC green-lighted my show I knew my budget wouldn't be as high as a million, and the May race was already fewer than twelve months away. Finding eligible cars isn't necessarily difficult, but coming up with an affordable one you want to drive is another thing altogether. I had no idea where to start looking.

For most of June I was up until three, four, even five in the morning searching the internet for contenders. Some nights I didn't go to bed at all. The mission to acquire a car completely took over my life. Weeks went by during which I was e-mailing people in America, Russia and Japan and getting back nothing other than astronomical price lists. I even roped in a fellow car nut, my mate Jay Kay, to give me a lift in his helicopter to go and look at a couple of cars in Lincolnshire. As soon as the dealer saw me arrive in a helicopter with a pop star and well-known car collector at the controls he was suddenly offering me a fantastic Maserati 150S for just £850,000. I test-drove it and it was great, but way out of my league. I also test-drove a Ferrari 195, which had done the Mille Miglia in 2004 and 2005, so it was eligible. It was in my price bracket too, which is to say it was under £300,000, but after the Maserati 150S it felt like driving my dad's old tractor. It looked good, but it wasn't right, so it was back to square one.

By August I was really starting to panic. The process of

filming bits and pieces for the programme had already started and I didn't have a clue about what I wanted to do the race in, never mind how to find it. The November cut-off for taking delivery of your car and completing the application with photographs and a full history was just ten weeks away. To make matters worse, it was in the back of my mind that the BBC thought I was already as good as in the race when actually, even if I found an eligible car I liked and could afford, there was no guarantee I'd be picked. The fact that on average two thousand people apply every year and only around 350 cars are accepted wasn't filling me with optimism. I could very well end up with a phenomenally cool and expensive motor with nowhere to drive it and no TV programme.

It was Nick Mason who suggested I enlist the help of a specialist car dealer. I was interviewing Nick for the programme because as well as being the drummer of Pink Floyd and an avid car collector, he's done the Mille Miglia twice. He pointed out that the classic car business is a small world and that dealers were the ones who knew it best. They knew what was eligible and where to find it. As it turned out, Nick couldn't have been more on the money if he'd been able to see into the future. His wise words were invaluable, and I am grateful.

After leaving Nick's incredible office, which was literally filled to the rafters with the coolest things imaginable – model F1 cars, real F1 cars, remote control planes, like a cross between Aladdin's cave and a toy shop – I went to see an old mate of mine, Paul Osborne, who runs a company called Cars International. In the past I'd bought two F3000 race cars from Paul as well as my Jordan F1, and I knew that he also had a few classics in his showroom. When I told him I was doing the Mille Miglia, he rolled his eyes. 'Scrapheap Challenge' he called it. I explained that I wasn't having much joy getting hold of a car for it and I could do with some help. He asked what my budget was, I said up to £300,000, and he rolled his eyes again because he knew that wasn't even slightly realistic. But he agreed to keep an eye out for me.

While Paul was out looking for cars, I was e-mailing him details of all the cars I was getting information about from all over the world. Having Paul on board proved instantly invaluable as he quickly went through this mountain of detail throwing out the donkeys. The list of possible contenders grew shorter and shorter.

By now, having looked around extensively, I was getting a better feel for what was out there and I told Paul that ideally I wanted something super rare, Italian and red. Paul pointed out that if I wanted rarity it was going to cost more money, and if I wanted something Italian it was going to be unreliable. (He was right on both counts.) He started sending me all these little red Italian sports cars, all around the £110,000 mark, but I just didn't like any of them. I couldn't say why, they just weren't right. I didn't have a specific car in mind, which was why it was hard to find something that took my heart. But I knew that I'd know it when I saw it.

Then, mid-October, Paul e-mailed me: 'Mate, I've got a

car. I've found one. It's the car.' And he was right. Paul had got advance warning of an estate sale, and among the lots was a red 1948 Maserati A6GCS. When I Googled it, the picture that came up on my laptop was exactly what I'd been after all along. It was a proper racing car, the kind Fangio would have chased Moss around the streets of Brescia in. Paul's e-mail informed me that it had been in the same family for 36 years (which gave it rarity value), it was red, and it was Italian. It was right.

It was also €750,000. I was straight on the online currency converter to work out what that was in real money and didn't much like the £495,000 it came back with. But Paul was very insistent, and added that if we were going to buy it we needed to move fast before all the other dealers heard about it.

It was then that I worked out that if I pooled all my resources I might be able to get together £200,000, not the £300,000 I'd always had in mind (to be honest, that figure had been a guesstimate from the outset), which of course left me with a £295,000 shortfall. I forwarded Paul's e-mail to my accountant with a note attached saying, 'What do I do?' Amazingly, my accountant found a bank willing to lend a chef over a quarter of a million pounds to drive a 60-year-old racing car through Italy at breakneck speed. We went to meet the banker in question who was very enthusiastic. He was into classic cars himself, said it sounded very interesting, and he was sure he could work something out. I said, 'Great, but you've only got 48 hours to decide.' He gulped, then he and my accountant went off, did the maths and came back with an offer on a loan with a lump sum at the end of it.

Then I panicked. What if the car needed a lot of work doing to it? There were bound to be expenses we hadn't considered. What about shipping and insurance and race suits and everything else I hadn't yet thought about? I was tying all my money up in the car; if anything went wrong, there was no contingency fund. So I got the paperwork couriered down, signed the deal, couriered it back, and the money was with Paul 48 hours later.

At this point I hadn't yet seen the actual car; all I'd seen was a picture on the laptop screen! While we were sorting out the money, however, Paul was getting the car checked out by the world's leading Maserati expert, Signore Adolfo Orsi Jr, whose family actually owned Maserati at one time. There is no one more knowledgeable than he is. Paul had also been on the phone to Maserati checking that the car was authentic. Maserati UK came back and said that if it was the car they had the details of, it was a very, very special car. They sent me a brochure produced by Maserati's historical centre in Modena. In the back was a list of all the races this car – my car, chassis number 2006 – had won. According to this document it was one of only three made in 1948 and it had been victorious in almost every race going. Yet while its sister cars had raced in the Mille Miglia, mine never had – a fact which I thought might just swing our entry. Either way, it was an amazing provenance. And then we got Signore Orsi's report, on twelve sheets of paper, each page signed by the man himself. In his opinion it was the genuine article, not a replica of any type. You can't really ask for more than that.

Two weeks later the car was delivered to Paul's workshop in Swindon. I shot up there, we pulled back the cover and just stood and stared in awe at it. I couldn't believe how immaculate it was. The bodywork was pristine, the paintwork was flawless, the whole thing was just perfect. But it was really uncomfortable when I sat in it. It had these bucket seats that were the tiniest I'd ever seen, designed for little Italian arses. It was really tight in there. My knees were hitting the wheel and I thought, 'There's no way I can drive a thousand miles in this.' The pedals were the wrong way round too, the brake and accelerator reversed: hit the accelerator and you stopped, hit the brake and you went flying. Paul assured me that wasn't a problem, it could be sorted out, and he told me that he'd fitted 7 foot American basketball players into Lamborghini Countaches over the years. 'Don't worry, we'll get you in this car.'

And then we fired it up. The noise was incredible, and the speed was intense. I drove it about 600 yards around this industrial estate and it was seriously quick. I pulled back in, then we spent the next two hours looking at it, going over all the bits and pieces that needed doing. Paul said that he'd put it through the workshop, strip it down, go through it with a fine-tooth comb, and that it shouldn't cost any more than £25,000. Fine. That I could handle. Not a problem. I went home and Sally cooked me an amazing meal. I love this girl.

Having got the car, and with Paul and his guys already working on it, my priority now was to get all the paperwork sorted out for the Mille Miglia organisers, which went smoothly. That wasn't the case with the V5 registration document. Until the car was registered in my name with the DVLA, the bank wouldn't release the funds for my loan. The bank had only given me a bridging loan to pay for the car, for which they were charging me £800 a week, and they would continue to do so until the car was fully registered in my name. It wasn't ideal, but the V5 would take no more than three weeks so I could live with it.

Four weeks later, still no V5 document. Five weeks later, still no sign of it. I called the DVLA in Swansea and was told that it was being processed and that they were very busy. The week after that, nothing. Eventually the V5 turned up, at the same time as a letter from the bank telling me that I owed them £9,800 in interest. I opened the V5, read it, and next to 'Make', instead of Maserati it said Fiat. I called Swansea and was told that it was my fault not theirs. I checked with Paul's guys: no, the form they took to the post office definitely said Maserati. It turned out that the person doing the paperwork in the post office had decided to re-brand the car.

By the time the DVLA had conducted their own independent investigation into what had happened, the V5 was 14 weeks late. I did a deal with the bank because it wasn't technically my fault, which brought the bill down from £25,200 to £18,000, but it was an expense with which I could have done without. As was the news from Paul's workshop that the car needed a full engine rebuild at an estimated cost of £40,000. With the £7,000 entry fee and the bill for shipping, accommodation, transport, insurance and crew mounting, it was all starting to add up.

There was some good news though. We managed to find a co-driver for the race, one who would actually fit in the miniature passenger's seat. I'm sure Paul went out specifically on the hunt for someone small, blonde and female, and in Sarah Bennett-Baggs he came up trumps, not least because she was a great driver in her own right (although if there's one thing I don't like it's German cars, and when we first went to meet Sarah she was racing a bright pink Porsche). Originally, Sally wanted to be my co-driver. I didn't fancy the thought of arguing all the way to Rome and back though, and I really wanted her to photograph the race, which just wasn't going to happen from the co-driver's seat of a 1948 Maserati travelling at 90 miles an hour. Anyway, Sally was so excited with her new camera gear and her up-and-coming photography business, so it was a great opportunity for her. My navigator Sarah would have preferred to be driving but she felt she could handle the navigation duties as well as anyone, she fitted in the car and we got on straight away, so she got the gig. So, with Sarah as my co-pilot and one of Paul's mechanics Simon heading up the support crew, at last it felt like the team was coming together, even if the car was still very much in bits.

In the end the engine rebuild cost £64,000. With spares impossible to buy, everything needed to be made from scratch. It required six new pistons at £3,000 each and two new gearbox cogs at £2,000 each. The new 18 inch water pipe took a guy six days to make at a cost of £1,600. The car had only four wheels, and as spokes are liable to break we thought it best to get another one made. One wheel: £3,000. As January rolled around the bills were coming in thick and fast.

There was a measure of relief in the form of an e-mail to the production company from the race organisers. There was no fanfare, no pomp and ceremony, just a very functional message saying that we needed to be in Brescia for 15 May for the start of the race. And with that one very businesslike message we were confirmed for the Mille Miglia. The first I heard was a text from the producer that read simply 'You're in.'

I was excited that we'd made it through, that the car had been chosen and that we were in the race, but more than anything I just felt relieved. All the hard work wasn't for nothing, we were going to have a TV programme after all. I'd be lying if I said there wasn't a split second of fear in there too. Now it was on, there was no going back. We were actually doing it. We had to get the car ready and to Brescia for 15 May and then I had to race the thing, which in itself was a scary thought. Hurtling down the road 4 inches off the ground in a car with 60-year-old brake technology is not for the faint-hearted. Every manhole cover and drain is a challenge, and anything less than absolute concentration will land you in a ditch. Modern cars are designed to get you from A to B efficiently and in comfort; this was designed just to get you from A to B as quickly as possible.

You feel vulnerable and exposed. That first time I drove it I got out wondering if this was such a good idea after all. It's a man's car, not a boy's car, and that's how you know it's a Mille Miglia car. It's a race for grown ups, not spoilt rich kids. That's what makes it special.

Four days before we were due to leave for Brescia, Paul threw a launch party at his showroom in South Kensington. He'd just bought Stirling Moss's Mercedes-Benz Gullwing, the one he did his reconnaissance laps in before going on to win the 1955 race, and along with the likes of Martin Brundle and Tony Jardine, Sir Stirling was there to look over my Maserati and give me some last-minute tips. Aside from my car suddenly springing a massive oil leak all over the courtyard and having to go back to the workshop in Swindon, it was a good evening. Sir Stirling said that he was concerned about the noise of my car, that Sarah and I wouldn't be able to hear each other over the engine. He gave me his business card and told me to e-mail him first thing in the morning and he'd organise some Peltor head-phones for us. I got home at three am and the first thing I did was send him the e-mail. I had Sir Stirling Moss's e-mail address. I wasn't going to wait until the morning to use it.

Oil leak fixed, the car was delivered to my place two days later for a final briefing and so that the production crew could start to fit cameras and recording equip-ment. Things quickly took a turn for the worse when the cameraman started to attach something that looked like a home video camera to the front of the car. I went nuts. Remember, this car had just cost me personally in excess of

£500,000 and this camera guy was trying to attach clamps and brackets all over the soft aluminium and perfect red paint with industrial sticky tape. I wasn't happy, and I wasn't having it. His suggestions that Sarah have a video recorder between her legs and that I clap a clapperboard every time we changed a tape were met with similar derision and shouts of 'Are you insane?' In the end I had a blazing row with just about everybody and threatened to pull out of the whole thing several times, before deciding that the best course of action was just to say yes to everything now and no when we got there and it was too late for them to argue about it. After everything that had happened and all that I'd been through to get this far, there was no way I was pissing about with this lot. I was going to race in the Mille Miglia, and that was all that mattered.

With everybody, including me, calmed down, the director said that there was one thing he wanted me to have: a radio. He said it was vital so that he and his film crew following in Range Rovers, on bikes and in a helicopter would be able to communicate with Sarah and me and tell us to slow down if they were having trouble getting shots.

I lost it again. I turned round, looked him square in the eye and said, 'Slow down? I'm sorry, mate, but I think you're missing the point.'

34 THE FINISH LINE

When we arrived in Brescia there was no fanfare to announce that the world's greatest road race was due to start there in three days' time. Not a poster, not a banner, not even a helpful signpost to tell entrants where they were meant to go on arrival. After a couple of minutes driving around we found someone to ask who pointed us in the direction of a huge, nondescript industrial estate that wasn't on any route map or the sat nav. When we pulled in there were only two other trailers parked in the car park. The place was like a ghost town. We parked up the trailer with the Maserati in it and went to the hotel for the night.

At ten o'clock in the morning we went back and it was like the busiest car park you've ever seen. The Mille Miglia seemed to have begun overnight; there were cars absolutely everywhere. Our little trailer was now next to a row of five lorries, none of which had been unloaded yet. We pulled down the shutters of the trailer and rolled the car out. It looked fantastic. Then they started unloading the lorry next to us, rolling out a beautiful sky blue Bugatti. Being rolled out of a trailer on the other side was a Porsche 550RSK, just like the one James Dean died in. Everywhere you looked there were gorgeous cars being unloaded and polished, millions of pounds' worth of super-rare cars being fired up and driven around. Never mind the world's greatest road race, we were literally standing in the world's most expensive car park.

Thinking that we wanted to beat the rush, we drove round the corner to hand in our paperwork, register and have the car scrutinised. The race official took one look at the documents we'd meticulously put together to ensure there couldn't possibly be any problems and said, 'Where's your VIFA certificate?'

The VIFA is a racing licence for the car to prove that it's an historic race car. We'd been explicitly told that we didn't need one, but the official was insisting that we did.

'Well, we haven't got one,' I said, 'and it takes four weeks to get one back in the UK, and the race is tomorrow. What do you want us to do about it?'

'Well, you need one,' the official replied. 'It's €125.'

Welcome to Italy. They do things differently there. If only the DVLA worked the same way.

Armed with a temporary VIFA certificate, we moved to the next station and got our number stickers (I was 161). When you do the Mille Miglia the driver also gets a fantastic free Chopard watch (I say free, but by this point I'd spent more than €18,000 on the entrance fee, accommodation and travel, so it was all relative). And once you've got your watch you take your paperwork to a little guy on the door and he gives you a tiny little sticker to put on the car windscreen. That little sticker means you're in, you're racing tomorrow, you're in the Mille Miglia.

We pulled the Maserati into this supersized warehouse where all the cars were lined up, and while Sarah and Simon our mechanic were sorting it out with fuel and giving it a last check over, I went for a bit of a wander to look at all these amazing machines in their neat little rows. That's when it really hit me. I was there, in Brescia, and I really was part of it. I looked around at all these incredible motor cars and in there with them was mine, ready for the start of the race. And this time I wasn't just going to be standing next to the start ramp, I was going to be on it.

Suddenly I found everything overwhelming. I was actually part of this event that I'd been dreaming of for the last 15 years. I remember thinking about all the years of hard work, all the hours and effort I'd put in to get there, what I'd had to do as a chef to arrive at a point where I could do this. It's not like I was a stockbroker who'd made it all on one deal and was straight in. I'd worked my nuts off all my adult life to be in this room, with these cars and these people in this race. Everything had been about getting to this moment. I was part of this peerless gathering and just being there made me feel special. Not important or arrogant, just special.

That night there was no organised dinner, no boozing or

laddish behaviour. We all just went back to our hotels and got an early night.

The next morning was organised chaos, and that's being polite. From the place where the cars were parked to the starting line in the centre of Brescia was about six miles, and even with police motorbike outriders leading the way and clearing a path it was a painfully slow and hot journey. The heat was a shock. We hadn't driven in anything like these conditions before, and as we snaked through the crowds in a convoy of 15 cars the thought of 1,000 miles of this didn't bear thinking about.

We pulled into the town, parked up, and suddenly thousands and thousands of people flocked around the car. The race was due to start that evening at seven pm, so we were there in the centre of town for the next four hours, apparently waiting for all the other cars to arrive, although it was hard to tell what was happening because there was no obvious logic to any of it. Instead of being parked in number or start time order, the cars looked like they'd just been dumped all over the city, anywhere there was a free space. Every street had yet more cars parked up it.

While we were waiting for all the other cars to arrive we received a phone call from the hotel to say that the headsets Sir Stirling Moss had arranged for us had arrived. But by then it was too late. Brescia was so full of people it would have been impossible for any of us to have made it to the hotel and back before the start. It was lovely of him to try though.

After a while we started to get a feel for the way it was

going to work. Rather than any clear instructions from the organisers, everything seemed to be working on a word-of-mouth basis. When the car in front of you moved, you moved and just hoped that the person in front of them knew what they were doing. When the guy next to me fired up his engine, I fired up my engine. In a thick German accent he said, 'We go now.'

I had no idea where we were going, but clearly we were heading in the right direction because pretty soon we were sitting in the world's biggest and most expensive traffic jam. There were tens of thousands of people swarming around the cars, and in the middle of all this mess the drivers were now pushing their cars slowly along because, unlike modern cars, these things can't handle traffic. They are essentially race cars, designed to go flat out, not to idle or crawl along. Constant stopping and starting does them in, so for the next two miles we were all on foot, pushing these vintage cars along the cobbled streets, none of us having the first clue about what was at the end of it. Everybody else was going that way so we were going that way too.

When the director finally found us he was going ape shit. 'You can't just go off like that!' he was shouting. 'You've got to tell us where you're going!' I told him we didn't know where we were going; it was up to him to keep up with us. We hadn't even started the race and already we were arguing.

We carried on pushing the cars for another couple of minutes until suddenly we rounded a corner and found ourselves in this great square full of people and grandstands and a ramp. Sarah suddenly got all excited. 'Is this the start, is this the start?' No one really seemed to know what it was, but the cars were now being divided. Some of them were going around the ramp, some were going over it. It was only as we got closer that we clocked that the cars going around the stand were the Aston Martins, the Porsches and the Mercedes, while the cars going up on the stand and receiving wild cheers and standing ovations from the crowd in the grandstand opposite were the Ferraris, Alfas and Maseratis. In Italy, only Italian cars are worthy of a round of applause.

When it was our turn, a guy came over, leaned into the car and attached a lead seal – the lead seal of Brescia – to the steering column. Then the car got blessed and we were directed up on to the ramp. As we pulled up onto it we appeared on the big TV screen, the crowd cheered, and we were then given our start time. Our Mille Miglia would start at 8.36 pm precisely.

While we were still on the ramp, an Aston Martin went the long way round, throttled it and roared up the road and off into the distance. It looked and sounded great, so as we pulled off the ramp I did the same. The rear wheels lit up, and as we blatted it down the ramp and up the street the crowd in the grandstand went wild.

Having been given our seal, a blessing and a start time, we parked up to get ready for the real start of the race. I'd had these race suits made for me and Sarah, based on the one Steve McQueen wore in the film *Le Mans*, but there was nowhere to change, so I slipped into mine in a shop doorway. Sarah didn't fancy getting undressed in the street so she disappeared, returning five minutes later in her race suit. I've no idea where she went.

Having looked at our itinerary, the director pointed out that there was a supper at the Mille Miglia Museum and said it would be a good idea to go. So we drove all the way out of town with a police escort, got to the museum, and instantly regretted it. The driveway of this place was absolutely bone dry and as we arrived in our beautifully polished car and brand-new spotless race suits we were engulfed in a cloud of dirt and dust. We looked like we'd already done the race twice, and to add insult to injury there was hardly anything to eat and nothing to drink but water. After a short stay we got back in the car and headed back to town and the start line.

We joined another queue of traffic and could see the start line half a mile away, straight ahead of us. Then we looked to our right and saw a little pizzeria outside which was parked the most amazing collection of clean and shiny vintage Ferraris, Astons and Maseratis. Clearly the drivers of these cars were the old hands who'd done this before and knew better than to bother with the supper at the museum. All these guys were coming out looking immaculate after treating themselves to a pizza and a nice glass of Chianti. We were hungry and covered head to toe in dirt.

At seven pm on the dot all the cars in this queue, none of which seemed to be in any kind of order, started moving towards the start. And suddenly, from all this chaos came a strange natural order. The cars may well have joined the queue for the start line randomly, but by some miracle of Italian organisation it was exactly 1 hour and 35 minutes from the time the queue started moving to when we got to the bottom of the ramp. Having slowly pushed the car along the road for the last hour and a half, we fired the engine up four cars from the ramp. Left and right there were thousands upon thousands of people. Three cars from the ramp, two cars from the ramp, then suddenly there we were, bang on 8:36.

As I pulled up I got so excited, and then completely focussed in on the clock, watching as it counted down. I was ready. My foot was hovering over the accelerator and my hand was gripping the gear stick, ready to quick-change it up – first, second, third. I was tense with adrenalin and nerves, but everything else – the build-up, the money, the pressure, the pomp, the circumstance – had just disappeared. I was there. I'd made it. That's all that mattered. Exactly one year earlier I'd been standing over there in the crowd, doing my piece to camera, wishing I was sitting behind the wheel of a beautiful old Italian sports car, about to head down the start ramp on my very own 1,000 mile adventure. Now, twelve months on, here I was.

As the clock hit zero and the starter dropped the flag I knew I'd achieved my dream. I'd never felt anything like it, and I'd gladly pay double to feel it again. As the flag went down I remember thinking that whatever happened next was a bonus. This was the moment that counted; this was what I'd worked so hard for all my life. From skateboarding round a Yorkshire farmhouse kitchen to crossing the start line of the Mille Miglia, this was what it was all about. The flag hit the floor, and then all I remember is first, second, third, and the noise of a hundred thousand Italians.

ACKNOWLEDGMENTS

James would like to thank the following people:

Everyone at HarperCollins for exciting times working on the new book: Jenny, Ione, Lizzy, Anna and Liz, and everyone else who helped out.

Special thanks to Dan for the endless hours of conversation. I think he knows more about me now than I do about myself.

Neale Haynes and the guys for getting some great photos for the cover.

Pippa and Chris, my left hand and right hand throughout my life.

All the girls at Limelight: Mary, Alison, Leonie, and especially my agent Fiona, who fill up my diary, but also help to fill up my garage.

Thanks to Paul for finding my Masa, and to Jonathan, Tim, Quinton, Micky, Mark and all the boys at both workshops for their work on all my cars.

Thanks to my family – Mum, Pete and my little sister – I love you guys so much.

And thanks to Sally, for being there through everything and for many happy years to come.

INDEX